The Fen

"Blachor's *Feminist's Guide to Raising a Little Princess* is a fun, informative read peppered with funny anecdotes and informative thoughts on things like the value of embracing the feminine, American optimism, and maternal health care. (There's also a chapter that will feel all too familiar to any parent who's ever taken their toddler to Disneyland Paris and immediately regretted it.) This is a book about what it means to be a feminist and trying to raise a feminist daughter who happens to be obsessed with the color pink, frilly dresses, and also being a princess. It's also about why you can't blame Disney. Even if you really, really want to."

—Jennifer McCartney, *New York Times* bestselling author of
The Joy of Leaving Your Sh*t All Over the Place

"I am pro-princess and became a staunch feminist (this combo is because of, not in spite of, my feminist mother). Devorah Blachor is a staunch feminist and became pro-princess (this is because of, not in spite of, her princessy daughter). Eventually, we both arrived at the same conclusion: the concepts are symbiotic, not mutually exclusive. In a world of toxic masculinity, knee-jerk reactions against princess culture are passé. Blachor's humorous guide helps parents surrender to the magic and find the right balance."

—Jerramy Fine, author of *In Defense of the Princess: How Plastic Tiaras and Fairytale Dreams Can Inspire Strong, Smart Women*

"Devorah Blachor deftly weaves personal stories with research and clever humor in *The Feminist's Guide to Raising a Little Princess*. This funny and relatable book is perfect for any imperfect parents who find things not going according to their parenting plans."

—Julie Vick, writer for the *Washington Post* "On Parenting" newsletter and *Parents* Magazine

"I happen to be the mother of a boy, but I have many friends who are both feminists and parents of pink-obsessed girls. I wholeheartedly recommend they read Devorah Blachor's *Feminist's Guide to Raising a Little Princess*. It's hilarious, wise, relatable, and insightful. I snort-laughed more than once while I read it. Before I even finished it, I started telling friends 'You have to read this book—you'll love it.'"

—Janine Annett, writer for *The New York Times Well Family* blog, *The Huffington Post*, and Parent.co

W9-CGV-441

"I adored Devorah Blachor's *Feminist's Guide to Raising a Little Princess*. It's a rare book that combines 'serious' science with hilarious 'opposite of serious' stories that bring the point of the 'serious' science home in a completely relatable way. For feminists with pink-and-princess-obsessed preschoolers who wonder where they went wrong, Blachor reassures you that it's not you—it's them! There's hard wiring that makes your child the way she is. I wish this book had been around when my daughter was small. I'll be sharing it with friends who are mystified by the little princesses in their own lives."
    —Page Barnes, editor and founder of *The Haven*

"I would call this book 'adorable' if I didn't think I'd get a punch in the nose. 'Genuinely funny,' 'hilariously inventive,' and 'truly insightful' work as well. With raw honesty, cynical wit, and even scientific research, Devorah has let us into her life as a mom who loves her daughter even as she is mystified by who the hell her daughter is. She exposes the real emotions as she competes for role-model dominance with Ariel, Cinderella, Elsa, and the whole gang of pink-loving Disney princesses. As a dad with a daughter who is constantly confusing me as well, I highly recommend this book. Even the footnotes made me laugh out loud. Don't miss them!"
    —Gary Rudoren, coauthor of McSweeney's *Comedy by the Numbers* and dad of twins

"The struggle is real. As a fellow feminist and mother of a young daughter, I too have battled the Princess Industrial Complex, but have been beaten down by tiaras and tutus. This hilariously funny book is a guide to tackling pink-glitter-bomb-fluffiness and #winning. Best of all, Devorah Blachor's commonsense talk teaches us how to counteract harmful messages while allowing our daughters to become their own people."
    —Fiona Taylor, cofounder of *The Belladonna*

The
FEMINIST'S GUIDE
to RAISING a
LITTLE PRINCESS

How to Raise a Girl

Who's Authentic, Joyful, and Fearless—

Even If She Refuses

to Wear Anything but a Pink Tutu

DEVORAH BLACHOR

A TarcherPerigee Book

tarcherperigee

An imprint of Penguin Random House LLC
375 Hudson Street
New York, New York 10014

Illustrations by Siobhan Gallagher

TarcherPerigee with tp colophon is a registered trademark of
Penguin Random House LLC.

Most TarcherPerigee books are available at special quantity discounts for bulk purchase
for sales promotions, premiums, fund-raising, and educational needs. Special books or
book excerpts also can be created to fit specific needs. For details, write: SpecialMarkets@
penguinrandomhouse.com.

LIBRARY OF CONGRESS CATALOGING-IN-PUBLICATION DATA
Names: Blachor, Devorah, author.
Title: The feminist's guide to raising a little princess : how to raise a girl
who's authentic, joyful, and fearless—even if she refuses to wear
anything but a pink tutu / Devorah Blachor.
Description: New York : TarcherPerigee, 2017. | Includes bibliographical references.
Identifiers: LCCN 2017012897 (print) | LCCN 2017034322 (ebook) |
ISBN 9781524704025 | ISBN 9780143130352 (paperback)
Subjects: LCSH: Girls. | Child rearing. | Feminism. | BISAC: FAMILY &
RELATIONSHIPS / Parenting / General. | SOCIAL SCIENCE / Feminism &
Feminist Theory. | FAMILY & RELATIONSHIPS / Life Stages / School Age.
Classification: LCC HQ777 (ebook) | LCC HQ777 .B55 2017 (print) |
DDC 649/.133—dc23
LC record available at https://lccn.loc.gov/2017012897

Printed in the United States of America
1   3   5   7   9   10   8   6   4   2

Book design by Sabrina Bowers

To my fabulous muses,
Cai and Mari

Contents

INTRODUCTION: How Many Feminists Does It Take
to Change a Lightbulb?   ix

PART 1:
The Little Princess Inside Our Home

CHAPTER 1: What Is a Little Princess?   3

CHAPTER 2: Who Are the Little Princess Parents?   25

CHAPTER 3: Mirror, Mirror, on the Wall, Who's the
Control-Freakiest of Them All?   53

CHAPTER 4: Congratulations! It's a *Beautiful*!   77

CHAPTER 5: The Magical World of the Disney Dollar   100

PART 2:
The Little Princess Outside Our Home

CHAPTER 6: Real Princesses Aren't Passive Cream Puffs   141

CHAPTER 7: Real Women Don't Cackle   163

CHAPTER 8: Do Real Princesses Do Windows?   175

CHAPTER 9: Feminist Fairy Tales   195

CHAPTER 10: Princess Perfect   208

CHAPTER 11: Love . . . Of Course! Love!   224

CHAPTER 12: Happily Ever After   238

AFTERWORD: Princesses and Wolves   265

ACKNOWLEDGMENTS   269

NOTES   271

ABOUT THE AUTHOR   275

Introduction

How Many Feminists Does It Take to Change a Lightbulb?

How many feminists *does* it take to change that lightbulb? The answer to the old joke is, "That's not funny!"

Here's another one: How many feminists with princess-obsessed toddlers does it take to change a lightbulb?

Answer: If we keep the room dark, perhaps no one will notice that my daughter looks as if a neon pink convertible has collided with a bubble gum factory and produced a rainfall of tulle, lace and tiaras.

That punchline is my life. When my daughter became obsessed with pink and princesses and all things girly, I wanted to keep the room dark. I was embarrassed. I still sort through her laundry in a baffled haze. Everything is pink: the tutus and the dresses, the sparkly, sequined T-shirts, the leggings with polka dots and the Disney underwear—each one with a different princess on it.

How did this happen? I ask myself. *I'm a feminist. I read* The Beauty Myth.

Once upon a time—and by "once upon a time" I mean before

I had kids—I had a clear[1] image of myself. Part of this image was that I would never have a pink-worshipping, frilly-dress-wearing, princess-obsessed daughter. How could I? When I was a little girl the story "The Ugly Duckling" spoke to me. Unattractive outcasts were my people, whereas princesses seemed to come from another dimension in which delicate alien beings flounced around with the lustrous hair I'd seen only in TV commercials. I identified with the ugly rather than the beautiful, with sparky sidekicks rather than submissive heroines. Princesses and everything that went along with them just weren't me—not as a nerdy schoolgirl and certainly not when I became an adult who favored oversized, frumpy clothing and wished the entire beauty industry would sink into the earth in a puff of silicone vapor.

But the joke was on me, because I had a child who was so obsessed with pink that 95 percent of her tantrums were actually about wearing pink clothing. The remaining 5 percent were about candy, but even those tantrums were sometimes about the failure of the candy to be pink.

So how *did* it happen? How did my parental aspirations collide with a color and a concept and take such a colossal beating?

The primary reason, of course, is that Mari really *wanted* to wear pink. But that sentence doesn't adequately convey what happened in my home. I'll try to illustrate what I mean with an equation.

Mari wanted to wear pink every day > I didn't want her to wear pink.

Now imagine that > (the "greater than" sign) is the size of the menacing snowman, Marshmallow, guarding the ice palace in *Frozen*. Got it? You're beginning to understand.

---

1 And deluded.

Mari wanted to wear pink and when this desire first surfaced she was a toddler. Her will was stronger than all the *Rocky* nemeses put together but without any stirring theme music playing in the background. And that's just an indication of how strongly she wanted to wear the clothing. It doesn't even begin to address her attraction to the princess characters and the dolls and the toys and the TV shows, the accessories and the jewelry and the costumes, the backpacks and the water bottles and the weird YouTube videos where that woman opens tubs of sparkly Play-Doh and mushes them into dresses for dolls and you only see her hands and her perfectly manicured Hello Kitty–painted fingernails.

The early years of childhood are hilarious, exasperating and challenging for all parents. When my daughter threw her pink and princess obsession into the mix, I knew that something had to give. It was her or me.

I chose to let something go. Mari's "Little Princess" stage was a chance for me to start a new stage too. There was a lesson to learn if I could only suspend my princess and pink resistance long enough to pay attention to more meaningful issues. There was an opportunity to figure something out about parenthood and my need to control.

There was also an opening to revisit the princess stories—both new and old—and reclaim the characters for myself and my daughter. I grew up with the docile, passive Disney princesses, but to my surprise there are twenty-first-century princesses who exemplify the exact qualities I hope to teach my daughter—resilience, authenticity, compassion and love. And they have come not a moment too soon.

I came to parenthood as a woman who'd spent years in and out of depression. I feared the consequences of becoming a mother, worrying how it might affect my mental state, my emotional health and the welfare of my children. But I could have never predicted how much the experience of being a parent would change me. Becoming a mother opened me up to love, to lightness, to connection and even to something I once thought about as the embodiment of the female problem: the color pink.

Having children also taught me that most precious skill—the ability to accept what comes along. Life definitely does not go according to plan. We can resist the children that come into our homes because they're not what we imagined or expected, or we can accept them.

So how does one achieve this alchemy of turning resistance into acceptance? Can it really be done, or is this just another fairy tale? Does one need wisdom, or a sense of humor? A glittery magic wand, or therapy? A child who refuses to leave the house without her organza rhinestone cape, or one who's satisfied just wearing the simple tiered and beaded mermaid ball gown?

All will be revealed in this book, and the story begins just as you might expect.

Once upon a time, there was a small and very cute princess-obsessed little girl, and a mother who learned how to Let It Go.

PART 1

The Little Princess Inside Our Home

Chapter 1

WHAT IS A LITTLE PRINCESS?

My Life in Pink:
THE SCIENCE OF LITTLE PRINCESSES

Mari and I are pretty attached. Like, maybe to an unhealthy degree. Here's why I think that happened:

When my son, Cai, was a baby, a babysitter came a few mornings a week so I could work part-time. Cai bonded with me, with his father, aka my husband, and also with the babysitter. She's a fabulous young woman who introduced Cai to her group of fabulous friends, and they showered him with adulation and attention. Cai loved a lot of people, and a lot of people loved Cai.

But when Mari came along, we had less money and by then I had ~~no career to speak of~~ less reason to return to work. For the first two years of Mari's life, the largest portion of her days was spent with me and my boobs. I'm still not sure which of us she loved more. She seemed pretty happy anyway.

Just before Mari turned two I had some freelancing opportunities, so we enrolled her in a half-day preschool program. On her first day when the parents left, all the kids cried. On the second day, most of the kids cried. On the third day, some of the kids cried, and the following week, none of the kids cried anymore. Except for Mari. She still cried when I left her, every day, ripping my heart out with each inconsolable sob.

Why was it so difficult for Mari? Maybe it was because the other toddlers lived near grandparents and relatives and were used to occasionally being without their mommies, while Mari had no such "extramaternal" experience. Or maybe it was because I was a crappy mother who'd raised an insecure emotional mess. It was probably one or the other.

I considered pulling Mari out of her program and giving up the idea of returning to work. But in time she started to settle, though it was definitely slow going. Mari was *that* kid—the one who's always on the teacher's lap in the photos they post on the preschool's Facebook page. She needed lots of attention and love, and she got it there. For that I'm very grateful.

She also started to get other ideas there. We'll address those soon.

Those were heady days. I'd drop Mari off at school and have *four free hours* to play around with. Man, was I elated, if elated means the same thing as insanely tired. Because Mari was also getting up very early to breastfeed. Did I forget to mention that? Mari was still breastfeeding and woke me every day at four a.m. to do it. It turned out she did like my boobs better than me.

We weren't doing it in public anymore. Mari breastfed before bedtime and naps and when she woke up, but she left my boobs alone for the rest of the day. If I had left it up to her she would have done it in public all the time, but at a certain point—I can't remember exactly when because of my sleep-deprivation-addled brain—I told her "Let's wait until we get home" and sometime after that, "Let's wait until bedtime." It worked because she hadn't yet passed the Psychotic Toddler Threshold.[1]

Here's a question. When Mari was a baby, I breastfed her in public with no reservation, shame or feelings of parental inadequacy. Once she hit toddlerhood, however, I felt uncomfortable whenever she wanted to nurse. Why is that? Why was my naked-boob-exposure awareness heightened just because Mari was a few months older? Why did I feel judged and critiqued for comforting my toddler, but didn't care when people disapproved of breastfeeding my baby in public? Discuss.

Back to my exhaustion, which was as deep and massive as Crater Lake, but without the stunning views and the gift shop. Too tired to think about anything other than sleeping, I decided to finally wean.

So there we were. Mari had just started preschool. I was trying to get her to give up the exact thing that comforted her most, and into this messed-up vortex of toddler separation anxiety, parental guilt and extreme exhaustion, something new and strange came into our lives. Something we had never really thought about before. Something that would change our lives forever.

It all started with Color Week.

What's Color Week? you say. *It sounds just adorable.*

Color Week was that thing where all the kids in Mari's preschool wore blue on Monday. On Tuesday, they wore yellow. On Wednesday it was red, on Thursday brown, and on Friday, all the kids dressed in either pink or purple—toddler's choice.

---

1 The Psychotic Toddler Threshold is the point at which your child makes the switch from a mild-mannered adorable little person to a being whose sole purpose is to make everyone around him or her miserable. Most toddlers are perfectly pleasant before reaching their PTT, which makes what comes afterward all the more perplexing.

Isn't that a fun way to learn about colors? Isn't that the sweetest thing ever?

For the purposes of this book, I took it upon myself to research which part of the brain processes color differentiation.

It's the occipital lobe, as I'm sure you all know already. The occipital lobe is one of the four major lobes of the cerebral cortex. In other words, this is your brain on color:

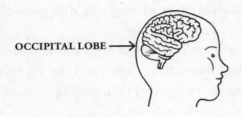

OCCIPITAL LOBE ⟶

Did you see that? No? Let me zoom in on that image for you.

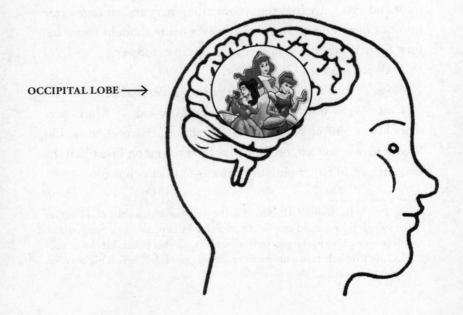

OCCIPITAL LOBE ⟶

I don't know if you can see what happened—it's very subtle—but it turns out that by stimulating the part of Mari's brain that recognizes color, a dormant predilection was aroused. Or implanted. It's a nature-versus-nurture thing—I'm still trying to figure it out. All I know is that Mari was forever changed.

Here's a helpful graphic to help illustrate the change in Mari's behavior.

BEFORE COLOR WEEK	AFTER COLOR WEEK
Me: Let's get dressed! **Mari:** Okay, Mommy.	**Me:** Mwaa mwaa mwaa, mwa mwa mwa. *(Because no matter what I said, Mari reacted in the same lunatic way since she'd already passed her Psychotic Toddler Threshold.)* **Mari:** NOT THAT ONE! NOT THAT ONE! THE PINK ONE! THE PINK ONE! NOT THAT PINK ONE! THE OTHER PINK ONE! I WANT THE OTHER PINK ONE! WAAAAAAAAAA!!!!!!

Sad to say, as soon as Mari became aware of the concept of color she began suffering from yet another new syndrome. This one was called PFD, a phenomenon discovered by Diane N. Ruble, Leah E. Lurye and Kristina M. Zosuls of Princeton University, the school where middle initials are a big thing. PFD stands for "pink frilly dresses." Here's what these developmental psychology researchers wrote in the *Princeton Report on Knowledge*, which is also known by its street cred name, P-ROK.[2]

> As researchers in the field of developmental psychology who study gender development, we have noticed that a large proportion of girls pass through a stage when they virtually refuse to go out of the house unless they are wearing a dress, often pink and frilly. The intensity of these desires and the extremity with which they are expressed has piqued our research interest. One young mother reported that her 3-year-old daughter could only be convinced to wear something other than pink when she was physically shown that *all* of her pink clothing was in the laundry. What is the driving force behind this phenomenon, which we call PFD?[3]

I know what you're thinking. That the mother whose daughter actually agreed to wear something that wasn't pink is one lucky bitch.

The researchers also point out that once children understand that there are two genders, identifying with their own gender becomes very important to them.

Did I mention that it was around this time that we let Mari watch her first movie? I didn't?[4] I'm just really forgetful sometimes, as I'll demonstrate again in about two seconds.

There you have it. All the facts have been laid out with supporting evidence submitted to the court. Now I ask the jury: What was I supposed to do? Get a two-year-old who had just started

---

2 They really do call it that.

3 This is an old-school footnote: D. N. Ruble et al., "Pink frilly dresses (PFD) and early gender identity," *P-ROK* 2, no. 2 (2007).

4 It was *Frozen,* as if you didn't know.

preschool to stop breastfeeding, stop biting,[5] and stop wearing her new favorite color all at the same time? It sounds like a sequel to *The Perfect Storm*, only much, much worse—kind of like the eternal winter storm that Queen Elsa set off in Arendelle.

So when Mari started demanding to wear only pink and became obsessed with princesses—a preference that generally occurs about five seconds after the pink fixation—we kind of let it happen. "Choose your battles," people sometimes say to parents, when what they really mean is "Please remove your child from the premises." We chose not to have this particular battle. In fact, sometimes we even enabled our Little Princess to flourish, as you'll soon see.

And so a Little Princess was born. Her name is Mari. May God grant me the serenity to accept the color pink, the courage to not let my house become a shrine to pink and princesses, and the wisdom to know that pink is just a color, not a decision to never attend college in the hopes of marrying wealthy.

Princess Studies 101: DO BRAINS EVEN MATTER?

Male and female brains are different. Duh!

—*Some guy in a bar*

So is it nature or nurture? In other words, are male and female brains different or are we more or less the same until we're born

---

5 Did I forget to mention that Mari was biting other kids?

and socialized into behaving according to what is expected and encouraged of our respective genders? Do some of us come out of the womb itching to design a hydraulic bridge, while others are predisposed to wearing puffy slippers with bear ears? How does this whole gender thing work?

At the end of the nineteenth century, scientists discovered that the male brain was bigger than the female brain. Because it was the olden days when most women were walking wombs instead of scientists and explorers and newspaper criers, many assumed that size must indeed matter. There was a consensus that women were intellectually inferior to men. Which was probably news to Marie Curie, the physicist and chemist who discovered two elements and won the same amount of Nobel Prizes.

Over time, scientific research bolstered the theory that women are dumber. For example, men consistently outperformed women on IQ tests. Until they didn't. Think about it. With your gendered brain.

The brain is mutable. It can and does change—the changes and development begin weeks after conception. While genes (nature) determine how the brain develops in utero, the environment— whether the mother is chronically stressed or smokes, for example— affects the brain's development as well. After birth, our life experiences play a role in shaping our brains. So if girls started to, say, I don't know, maybe go to school or college or something for the first time, then it would certainly affect how their brains developed. Harvard, which was founded in 1636, claims to be the first institution of higher education in America. The first university to admit women, however, was Oberlin College *two hundred years later*.

If the brain changes according to environment and women didn't have access to basic education or higher education, then men outperforming women on IQ or other intelligence tests isn't convincing proof of intellectual superiority. What you need to do is allow women that access and then let their brains and their daughters' brains and so on through their granddaughters' granddaughters' brains develop and connect according to the new set of circumstances. And *then* test their IQs.

Like in 2012. That's when women outperformed men on IQ tests for the first time. The findings were authored by James Flynn, who studied IQ so much that he got something really cool named after him. ("The Flynn effect" refers to the overall increase in IQ scores since the 1930s.) The brain is so fluid—and neuroscientists are only beginning to discover the depths of its plasticity—that it's still hard to draw convincing conclusions from any one study.

Intellect aside, men and women do seem to be different from each other, and there has been a ton of research designed to discover brain differences between the genders. Our survey says that men and women generally have amygdalae that behave differently— this is the part of the brain associated with stress, emotional responses and sexual arousal—because amygdala activity and responses to stimuli vary according to gender. And while men have larger brains, women might use their brains more efficiently. Women also have a higher proportion of gray matter and lower proportion of white matter than men. But what does all this mean? Also, does matter even matter?

And here's an even more confusing thought: What if we've been asking the wrong question all along?

The faulty question is: What are the differences between the male and female brains? The assumption is that male and female brains are distinct.

In 2015, Professor Daphna Joel of Tel Aviv University led a

study that examined the brain scans of 1,400 people aged thirteen to eighty-five. The study found that while some brain features are more common in one gender or the other, when you look at the whole study, very few people—between 0 percent and 8 percent—actually have a brain that is fully male or female. In other words, our brains are not one or the other. We're all a little bit country, and a little bit rock 'n' roll. Tell us about it, Professor Joel:

> Here we show that, although there are sex/gender differences in brain and behavior, humans and human brains are comprised of unique "mosaics" of features, some more common in females compared with males, some more common in males compared with females, and some common in both females and males. Our results demonstrate that regardless of the cause of observed sex/gender differences in brain and behavior (nature or nurture), human brains cannot be categorized into two distinct classes: male brain/female brain.[6]

Does that blow your mind a little? Daphna Joel concludes that it's meaningless to talk of a brain as being female or male. "Brains are intersex—a mix of male and female characteristics," she says.

So yes—Mari and the legions of princess-obsessed little girls have been socialized to like pink. There's no doubt about that one.

But here's a question whose answer I still don't know: Like white and gray matter, does pink matter? If my daughter dresses in pink every day and surrounds herself with it and even begs to be bathed in it—because, needless to say, someone invented pink bath bombs shaped like cupcakes—will all this pink have an adverse effect on her? Unlike the secrets of the brain, which I'll

---

6 D. Joel et al., "Sex beyond the genitalia: The human brain mosaic," *Proceedings of the National Academy of Sciences* 112, no. 50 (2015).

leave to Daphna Joel and her peers, I'm still trying to figure that one out. That's kind of what this book is about.

Opposite of Serious

Most Little Princesses start out as Little Princess Toddlers. If you're concerned that your daughter might be a Little Princess Toddler and you wish to seek help before it's too late, the first step is to have her take this helpful diagnostic quiz. Everything will soon become as clear as an Arendelle ice crystal.

Quiz:
Are You a Little Princess Toddler?

1. *On most mornings you can be found:*

   A. Snug in your parents' bed with your fingers in your mother's nose and your heel digging into your father's neck.

   B. Removing your princess Pull-Ups so that you can pee on the floor.

   C. Waking up your family with a demand to bake cupcakes without delay.

   D. Taking off the tights that took your mother five minutes to get you into, because they're not the correct shade of magenta.

2. *During snacktime you:*

   A. Chew one of your apple slices, spit it out onto the floor and then crumble your cracker into your mother's special drink.

B. Refuse to even look at an edible item unless it's in the drinkie yogurt food group.

C. Hit your older brother on the head with your sippy cup.

D. Sing "Let It Go."

3. *At bedtime, you like to:*

A. Demand to read the very book that has mysteriously disappeared without a trace.

B. Jump up and down on your older brother's bed and insist on sleeping with his security stuffed tiger.

C. Drink large quantities of water, take off your princess Pull-Ups and then pee on your sheets.

D. Ask to brush your teeth and then cry because you threw your Aurora toothbrush in the toilet and now have to use a generic one until a new princess toothbrush can be procured.

4. *When strangers meet you, they say to your mother:*

A. What a little angel you have!

B. Don't worry—it's just a phase.

C. You look tired.

D. I've never seen that shade of pink on something that wasn't Jennifer Lopez.

5. *When you enter a supermarket you generally tend to:*

A. Realize you have to pee.

B. Wait until you're close enough to the wine display to start grabbing.

C. Point to random passersby and say, "You're a monster!"

D. From thirty feet away, spot sugary crap with a princess image on it and scream until it's purchased.

6. *During your mother's Skype interview to return to work and prove to herself that she can be a useful member of society again, you:*

A. Take off your clothes, enter the room and announce that you need to poop.

B. Enter the room and bite her leg fiercely so that she shrieks "What the fuck!" at a decibel level that causes the interviewer to suffer from temporary deafness.

C. Stand outside the door and say, "Mommy Mommy Mommy" ten thousand times.

D. Cause an electrical short in the house by inserting the arm of your Elsa MagiClip doll into an electrical socket.

7. *Your favorite T-shirt has the image of:*

A. Bob the Builder.

B. Winnie the Pooh.

C. Caillou.

D. If you try to give me a T-shirt or any other item of clothing that's not a dress, I will suck all the remaining joy from you for the rest of the day.

8. *The only pair of shoes you agree to wear have:*

A. Lights that go on and off.

B. Eyes and ears so that your feet resemble little bears.

C. A strap and buckle combination that is so complicated to negotiate that your mother needs two special drinks to unwind after putting them on.

D. Bows, flowers, sequins, fluffy bits, high heels and a matching handbag.

9. *When your brother is talking about Minions you:*

   A. Say, "Macaroni, spaghetti, meatball," and then you both giggle.

   B. Shoot him with a lipstick taser.

   C. Discuss Steve Carell's oeuvre.

   D. Scream: *IT'S MY TURN TO TALK ABOUT* FROZEN*!!!!!*

10. *Yesterday, you made the following demand that made your parents look sad, angry and helpless all at once:*

   A. I want another treat.

   B. I want to watch *Teletubbies*.

   C. I want to take off my clothing in this public place where there are people who clearly don't like children.

   D. I want you to hire the Disney Collector lady to perform at my bat mitzvah in nine years.

11. *Your favorite holiday is:*

   A. Christmas because of all the love you feel flowing around you.

   B. Halloween because you get to dress up.

   C. Labor Day because you identify with the workers. Wait, what?

   D. Wassailia. Look it up, bitches.

My Life in Pink:
WHO'S AFRAID OF PRINCESSES?

Me, that's who.

I even hated the Disney princesses a little bit.

That's bananas, you're probably thinking. *What have they ever done to you?*

It's a fair question. At first, they look pretty innocent. None of the Disney princesses has ever hit a puppy, as far as I know. They're not lobbyists trying to overturn *Roe v. Wade.* They're not responsible for me never having fulfilled my secret dream of living in Barcelona, and they've never even run a Ponzi scheme to defraud elderly people out of their savings. So what was my problem?

It started, of course, when I watched the Disney princess movies for the first time as a little girl. I liked them. I liked *Bambi* much more, but the princesses were okay. I never fantasized that I was a princess, however, or dreamed that I'd become one. Still, in spite of my apathy I know the princesses affected me. Because once I got older, I waited for my prince to come.

And waited.

And waited.

And waited.[7]

But this isn't about how there were no good men. This is about how I waited because I was certain I'd eventually find the perfect boyfriend who would become my ideal husband. That was the fairy-tale narrative.

---

7 *And I know it's totally crazy to think I'd find romance!* If you don't get that song reference, then you have probably picked up this book by mistake. I'm so sorry about that.

It so happens that it was also the narrative of my Jewish education. In Judaism, there's a concept called *bashert.* Our teachers taught us that everyone has a *bashert*—roughly translated as "meant-to-be." If we were good, we were told, our *bashert* would come along, if not on horseback then hopefully at least with a law or a medical degree. Even more important than his wage-earning potential, he'd be the exact right man for us—the yang to our yin—and we'd live happily ever after.

As this story was being sold to me both in the movie theater and at school, I played it safe. I spent my childhood being good and chaste and having faith. At fifteen, I was lonely, but I believed it would all work out. At twenty, I was very lonely yet still believed that my prince would come. At twenty-five, I despaired because everyone I knew had been in a serious relationship except for me. I was also still a virgin,[8] and that made me feel like a freak that no one would ever want.

Was my decade of loneliness the fault of the princesses? More to the point, should I sue Disney for $179 billion?

Let's examine the evidence. I'm forty-five. When I refer to "princess movies," I mean the trio I grew up with—*Snow White*, *Cinderella* and *Sleeping Beauty*. If Disney princesses have a reputation for being passive cream puffs, it's because of these three dull, uninspiring icons. I dare you to call these characters "heroines" with a straight face. Two of the princesses literally sleep through parts of their story.

And no wonder. When the three films were made, Disney was decidedly unreconstructed. In terms of feminism, this was a sleepy period. Women got the right to vote in 1920, and then the

---

8 So maybe I was a Disney princess after all!

"feminist timeline" is relatively bare until the second wave of feminism hit in the 1960s. (In 1957, the numbers of women and men voting were approximately equal for the first time. There's probably a connection between that and the resumption of feminist achievement, but that discussion is way too serious for a book about Little Princesses.)

For Mari, these early films were beside the point. She saw *Snow White* a few months after seeing *Frozen* and forgot about it the next day. She began loving princesses long before she'd seen any of the films—though she instantly loved Aurora more than Cinderella because her hair is flowing while Cindy's is in a bun, and because Aurora's dress is *pink*.[9] In Mari's eyes, just the concept and appearance of the princesses was enough to inspire her. The actual stories are irrelevant to Little Princesses.

But, embedded as they are in our culture, the stories *did* matter to me. Even though I never loved the movies like my "girly-girl" sister did, they got under my skin. Like many women, I learned that being beautiful mattered. I learned that a prince can save you. Thanks to my religious education, I also learned that to get said prince, one only had to be good.

And so I waited and was alone for many years. Unsurprisingly, I was also clinically depressed. There's a connection there. A passive approach to life—where you depend on outside forces instead of your own resources—is often correlated with depression. In other words, since their princess movies promoted the passivity I'd embraced, I *should* sue Disney for emotional distress, right?

Unfortunately my cunning plan to bathe myself in pink

---

9 Pink trumps everything, in case you haven't been paying attention.

diamonds is flawed. Aside from the fact that its legal team would be far superior to mine,[10] suing Disney, or blaming Disney for anything that happened to me, is just another symptom of passivity. In my midtwenties, the only way for me to climb out of my depressive state was to take responsibility for my life. No one was to blame for my being alone except for myself, my actions, my inaction and my inability to open myself up. Once I accepted this, I started to let men into my life. None of them were princes, but some of them were okay. I even married one eventually. He doesn't wear satin gloves or ride a horse, but he does massage my feet, so I think I've gotten a pretty good deal. Don't tell Disney about him, though, because I might change my mind about the lawsuit and foot massages might turn out to be admissible evidence in court.

◆ ◆ ◆

Interesting Little Princess Fact #1

Like many girls her age, Mari actually started talking about princesses before she ever watched a princess movie. Many people attribute this preternatural knowledge to preschool attendance. When girls see other girls with their princess backpacks, princess water bottles, princess tattoos and princess face piercings, they realize that they've been missing out on this essential part of their childhood.

However, once she did start watching princess movies, I had the opportunity to revisit them for the first time since I was a little girl. Watching *Snow White* with Mari constitutes the most

---

10 Particularly as I don't have a lawyer.

boring eighty-three minutes of my life, ever, and that includes the curling finals of the 1998 Winter Olympics.

Yet I remember liking *Snow White* as a child and have no explanation other than that *Star Wars* forever changed cinema and will prevent another *Snow White* from ever happening again. Thank you, George Lucas.

✦ ✦ ✦

My Life in Pink:
THE MANY WAYS TO DISLIKE CINDERELLA

Let's see if you've been paying attention, with this brief Little Princess Pop Quiz. Everyone pick up your pencils.

QUESTION: Why are the early Disney princesses—aka the Sleepy Trio—so passive?

ANSWER: Because they need a man to save them, of course.

Now, it's one thing for writers to have spun that fool's gold back in the day when vacuum cleaners were marketed as a perfect Christmas present for the ladies. But the fairy-tale theme in cinema persists. Isn't that a bitch? Or at least a wicked witch?

And our three waiting ladies are hardly alone in their male-centered orbits. In 1985, American cartoonist Alison Bechdel introduced a character who refused to watch a movie unless:

A. It had at least two women in it

B. who talk to each other

C. about something besides a man.

The "Bechdel test" caught on and is now used to illustrate how film and TV fail to meet the criteria again and again. A

Bechdel analysis of 2013 blockbusters concluded that seventeen out of fifty films passed the test.[11]

Here's something I—and by I, I mean Reese Witherspoon—said in an *Elle* interview:

> I started noticing a couple years ago that I wasn't seeing women as the stars of movies. I'm seeing them as the guys' girlfriends, or so-and-so's wife. I just thought: "God, if I don't start buckling down and start producing some movies, what's my daughter going to see in the movies?"

Sadly for Reese's daughter, and for mine, they will get to see not just one Disney version of *Cinderella*, but two. In 2015 Disney released a live-action version of *Cinderella*. I realize there's only so much you can do with the plot of a folktale that has ancient origins, but at the same time, did Disney really have to stick with the 1950 version so closely? There are multiple ways to dislike the original Disney movie.[12] Here are just a few of my favorites:

> Once upon a time, three mean and ugly women victimized a young, pretty one.

Or how about this one?

> Once upon a time, a young woman's beauty solved absolutely all her problems.

Here's a perplexing one:

> Once upon a time, a handsome prince fell in love with a beautiful woman, but he couldn't recognize her without her

---

11 The analysis was done on Vocativ.com and the point of the article was that Hollywood could make more money if it passed the test more often. *Frozen* passed the test.

12 *Cinderella* 2015 was even worse than the original. We'll get to that in chapter 7.

fancy clothes and had to ascertain her identity using her shoe size. *Wait, what?*[13]

Although, arguably, the one that messes girls up the most is this:

> Once upon a time, a woman was in distress. Once she got the Ring, however, she never had to worry about anything ever again. It's all about the Ring.

On that note, I'll just go ahead and quote Reese Witherspoon again. Here's what she said to the *New York Times* about her film *Wild*, based on the memoir by Cheryl Strayed:

> We save ourselves. Every woman knows it.

Yes, we do. It took me a little too long to figure that out. Besides waiting for my prince, I also waited to get help for depression, waited to figure out what was holding me back and waited to take responsibility for my own life. Once I did, it started turning out all right. Spoiler alert: There was absolutely no ring involved.

We save ourselves. The clock just struck midnight. So unless we can retell the story in a relevant way, let's put Cinderella to rest. It's time.

Little Princess Pie

Little Princesses usually happen when parents of toddlers get distracted by other priorities, just at the very moment when a percentage of girls begin obsessing about pink. This pie chart is

---

13 That line should immediately make you think *Frozen*, because if you're reading this book you've probably seen it more times than you can count. If you haven't seen *Frozen* and you have in fact picked up this book by accident, then once again I am so, so sorry.

the first in a series that analyzes the breakdown of how parental attention is manipulated into allowing the home to become a shrine to princesses and pink.

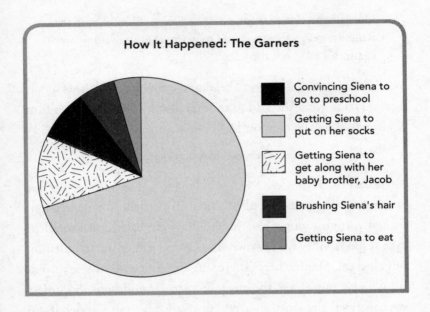

In our first case study, we see that Siena's parents devote considerable time to making sure Siena doesn't mutilate her baby brother, Jacob. Siena also must be coaxed to go to preschool. The biggest energy suck for the Garners, however, is getting Siena to put on her socks.

"Why would someone be so resistant to putting on socks?" Siena's father has said on multiple occasions.

As you can see, the Garners have no remaining energy to combat the influence of Little Princess culture, which explains why Siena became a certified "LP" just minutes after her third birthday. Sadly, the Garners also have little energy to get Siena to eat, which is why she subsists on drinkie yogurts and crackers.

Chapter 2

WHO ARE THE LITTLE PRINCESS PARENTS?

My Life in Pink:
MORTIFIED FEMINIST MEETS THE ENABLER

I went to an all-women's college where feminism was only slightly less popular than the Indigo Girls. I was already thinking about feminist issues because I grew up in a traditional community where the women were always the homemakers and often worked outside the home as well, whereas the men still didn't know how to locate the electric can opener sitting in plain sight on the countertop.

I don't blame the men. I blame the women for buying electric can openers. No, I don't. Blame is one of those things that saps our energy and since we have small children, none of us has energy to spare.

It did bother me, though—seeing the women working so hard in roles where they were generally underpaid, undervalued and underappreciated. I knew the system was wrong, and then I went to this university where the goal of gender equality was sacrosanct. By the time I graduated I was most definitely a feminist.

I still am.

Which makes Mari and her Little Princesshood all the more distressing.

I dressed her, of course, in gender-neutral baby clothes—mostly hand-me-downs from her brother, Cai. All her dolls were of the stuffed animal variety, with nary a voluptuous blond-haired plastic bombshell in sight.[1] My language was also mostly gender neutral and my husband, Matt, agreed to start wearing a kilt around the house.[2]

In light of all my fabulous feminist efforts, I expected that Mari would respond. I had other expectations too. When I found out I was pregnant with a girl, I instantly had an image of the child she'd become. Like Cai, she'd be dark haired, introspective and calm.

Ha-ha-ha-ha-ha-ha-ha-ha and countless additional "ha's" that can't possibly fit on this page.

Man plans and God laughs. Women have feminist intentions and Disney is valued at $179 billion. Mari is blond and outgoing and just putting the word "calm" in the same sentence with her name is making me do that weird thing with my face where I scrunch up my nose and look like I've just smelled wet dog.

She most definitely did not turn out the way I expected. And whose fault is that? It's mine, for having expectations in the first place. Expectations are the enemy of inner peace. Did you know that? The more you let them go, the better off you'll be.

---

1 Sounds like a weird sex toy.
2 Matt is Welsh, not Scottish. Also I'm lying about the kilt.

I understand that now, and I'm doing my best to give Mari room to be who she wants to be, stopping short of buying her all the toys that Disney Collector recommends.[3]

Still, I can't help but be embarrassed by the whole thing. When Mari and I go out on the town—like, say, to the pharmacy—and she's wearing a hot pink shirt and her sequined watermelon tutu and her fuchsia tights and glittery Princess Sofia shoes, I wonder what people are thinking. That I'm a bad mother? That *I'm* the one who's pink obsessed?

I know, of course, that most of them are probably thinking this: *Damn it. I forgot to get the milk. Now I have to go all the way back to the store and check out again. Why didn't I take a list with me? Why is that little girl crying? Maybe if I walk fast enough, I can get out of earshot of that crying child. Why is her mother wearing those ill-fitting beige pants?*

Clearly I'm no good at trying to figure out what strangers are thinking. Instead I'll do something useful, like categorize the three types of Little Princess parents. Here they are:

1. The Mortified Feminist

2. The Enabler

3. The Dad

---

3 Ooh—that Disney Collector! With her perfect pink flower fingernails, and her flawless Hello Kitty fingernails, and her impeccable Princess Belle with butterfly fingernails. I mention her a lot in this book, which should make perfect sense to anyone with a Little Princess in their house and YouTube access.

The Mortified Feminist

As I've demonstrated, I'm a Mortified Feminist. When people see my daughter in her finest fancy, frilly frock, I say things like, "Isn't she hilarious? She insisted on wearing that!" I want the person who's been blinded by hot magenta to understand that I would have made different clothing choices for my daughter, and that a woman should *not* earn only seventy-eight cents for every dollar earned by a man.

Some people nod their heads in commiseration when I start on my whole "I'm not the one who's pink obsessed" spiel while others are bored silly and find an excuse to walk away. Still others are offended by my approach.

I don't get it. These people—the ones who are offended—claim that I, and women like me, are sucking the fun out of fairy tales and girlhood. "Let girls be girls," they say. "Why do you hate everything that's feminine?"

It's true that feminists might have a complicated relationship with femininity, but get in line. We're all trying to figure it out. I'm certainly not hostile toward feminine qualities such as empathy and being nurturing. Not only women should embrace any positive feminine tendencies they have—men should cultivate them too, as much and as often as possible. We'd all be a lot better off, no?

But when I see Mari flipping out over pink and observe how much attention she gets for it—and we'll get to that soon—it makes me stop and wonder where it's all going.

When I walk into a toy store and one half of the store is entirely pink and includes an extensive cosmetics section, an accessories section and a princess section that would make Cinderella stick her finger down her throat and pretend to hurl, it leads me to believe that the pink thing has gone too far.

Also—and sorry if I'm offending anyone but I'm going out on a limb here—I just think that maybe the Elsa Glitter Glider MagiClip doll, the Elsa Musical Magic singing doll and the Elsa classic 12" doll ought to be enough. Does the world really need an Elsa Ice-Skating doll?

The Enabler

Little Princess Enablers are parents who actually go out to buy their Little Princesses pink dresses, frilly accessories and pink and princess-themed toys. Isn't that terrible? Aren't Little Princess Enablers the *worst*? I mean, how irresponsible can you be? Isn't it enough that . . . What's that? Why am I being such a bitch? It seems like I'm so over-the-top with my antienabler shtick that I must be hiding something? What are you implying?

What?!

How dare you!

I am not. I'm not, I say. Stop badgering me. Where did you get that blinding strobe light? Which one of you is the good cop? Okay, okay! Yes, it's true. I'm a Little Princess Enabler!

Oh, God. I feel so much lighter now that I've admitted that. Get the handcuffs[4] and I'll tell you exactly how it happened.

A few months after Mari started preschool, she bit another kid. I can't say I was shocked. She bit me occasionally. She bit Matt and Cai sometimes as well. She started biting before she even understood it caused pain. But by then she was two and

---

4 More sex toys!

she understood that people didn't like being bitten and she still did it. She soon bit a second kid in her program and then a third.

The preschool teacher was terrific, meeting with me and Matt and trying to figure out ways to "wean" her from the biting. There were other kids biting as well—Mari came home once with a bite mark on her arm that looked as if a dog had attacked her—but she was doing it more than others.

We started using a sticker chart whereby Mari earned a smiley face whenever she used "gentle hands." In toddler language, "gentle hands" means you didn't bite anyone, scratch them, pull their hair or shove them—at least not while the teachers were watching.

Toddler aggression, incidentally, is considered a normal part of toddler development and usually ends by age three to three and a half. We eventually discovered this encouraging statistic, though it didn't help us at the time. Mari wasn't even two and a half when she started biting other kids. We had a long wait ahead of us.

I was embarrassed to face the other mothers. Some of them were kind and compassionate. "One of my kids also went through an oral phase," one told me after Mari had bitten her son's back. But another mother—whose daughter was also biting—decided that Mari was trouble. She started calling all the parents and collecting stories about Mari. Once she'd completed her dossier, she presented it to the preschool teacher and demanded that something be done about Mari.

When I heard about this, I felt so sad. The idea that there was a person out there in the world who had it out for my daughter, who was actually spending her free time talking about Mari in this way and with such bad intentions toward her, made me understand how vulnerable Mari really was, and how much she needed me to protect her. That knowledge comes with pain, because as parents, we know we're not always going to be able to protect our kids.

This experience of feeling that Mari was being attacked touched something deep inside me. Along with swirling sadness, I felt an enormous surge of love for her. And despite all my grumbling about how much I hated her princess obsession, in the midst of my deepest funk, I went out and bought her this:

Mari's first princess castle.
(Photo credit: Confused Mother)

Why did I do that?

For the reason that precipitates the downfall of all parents.

I just wanted to make her happy.

I know that's messed up. Mari doesn't need toys to make her happy. She needs my love. This is what's called a "parenting fail." It wasn't my first and it won't be my last. In fact, that same day, I also bought her this:

Mari's first princess dress.
(Photo credit: Very Confused Mother)

A few months later, Mari finished her first "gentle hands" sticker chart. Of course no one is keeping score, but it so happens that she kicked her biting habit months before the daughter of the "do something about Mari" mother.

I was proud of her. We asked her what she wanted as a present and, without hesitating, Mari said, "I want to go to the mall-ie and buy a new dress." Here's what she chose:

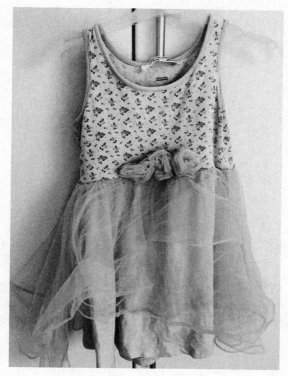

Mari's second princess dress.
(Photo credit: Indulgent and Extremely Confused Mother)

And that summer, while visiting my parents, Matt and I pulled into their driveway and spotted something pink across the street. The neighbors were having a garage sale. Like zombies, we crossed the sleepy suburban road and paid $10 for this:

Mari's third princess dress. (Photo credit: Mother Whose Apartment Living Has Left Her Woefully Unprepared for the Lure of Garage Sales)

Why on earth did we do this? I still don't know. As enablers, we know not what we do.

So, with all these princess dresses—purchased by me and not by unreconstructed relatives who think princesses are worthy obsessions for little girls—I have to ask, am I still a feminist?

I am.

But I'm also a mother. I have weak moments and strong ones. I have moments I'm not proud of and others when I think I nailed it.

When I bought Mari those dresses, I wasn't at my best. But I wasn't at my worst, either.

And when I taught Mari to recognize the letter "M," and when I convinced her it was better to run around in the park in sneakers rather than to limp along in her play high heels—were these my best parenting moments? Nope. Not them, either.

So when *am* I at my best as a mother? It's not when I'm a faithful feminist or a lapsed one. It's not when I have the energy to say no to an intensely willful child or when I surrender to her demands like a tired, guilt-ridden, coddling parent.

I have no doubts about this one: I'm at my best as a mother when I feel the love flowing unfettered between Mari and myself. Because when it flows, it really doesn't matter what color we're wearing.

Three little princess dresses having a nap.
(Photo credit: Tired Mother)

The Dad

The Dad is an enabler with a penis. At least, he is in our home. The Little Princess Toddler Dad is the guy who goes to the store to get a toilet rim block and comes back with the one that has pink liquid inside it because he knows it will make his daughter happy. I wish I was making this up. We have pink toilet rim blocks.

Opposite of Serious

In this segment we explore how the three Little Princess Toddler parent types react in different situations.

1. *Princess Toddler has just watched video of Disney Collector playing with the Princess Ariel Water Palace bath playset with the Fairytale Float Ariel doll, featuring Elsa and Anna on homemade floats. She wants to watch another one, but it's bedtime.*

What Would They Do?

Mortified Feminist: While putting toddler to sleep, praises the homemade flotation device that enabled Elsa and Anna to float even though they aren't semiaquatic like Ariel. Notes that objects float when they are less dense than the fluid in which they are sitting.

Enabler: While putting toddler to sleep, agrees to have another princess bath party the following day after purchasing Fairytale Float Belle and Rapunzel dolls.

Dad: Lets toddler stay up and watch MagiClip Fairytale Wedding after agreeing to buy floating Belle and Rapunzel dolls *and* a Sofia the First 2-in-1 Sea Palace playset.

Jesus: Expresses sadness about all the merchandising aimed at young children.

2. *Princess Toddler refuses to get dressed because her favorite tulle tutu is in the wash.*

What Would They Do?

Mortified Feminist: Lets her wear the dirty tutu.

Enabler: Suggests wearing a tiara that day to offset the loss of the tutu.

Dad: Gives her the new princess dress that was supposed to be a Christmas present.

Jesus: Expresses sadness about all the wars.

3. *Princess Toddler is twirling in front of the mirror, singing "Let It Go."*

What Would They Do?

Mortified Feminist: Tries to find her old Helen Reddy cassette.[5]

Enabler: Takes a video and posts it on Facebook.

---

5 When she can't locate the cassette, she finds the song "I Am Woman" on YouTube and discovers that Helen Reddy is wearing the pantsuit version of Queen Elsa's glittery green gown. Google it, bitches.

Dad: Puts *Frozen* in the DVD player, even though bedtime is in ten minutes.

Jesus: Expresses sadness about Hans's betrayal.

4. *Princess Toddler is inconsolable because there are only white marshmallows left in the package.*

What Would They Do?

Mortified Feminist: Asks, "What's the difference?" and agrees to give her three pink gummy bears to avoid the tantrum.

Enabler: Agrees to give her three pink gummy bears to avoid the tantrum and then paints her toenails afterward.

Dad: Agrees to give her a bucket of pink gummy bears to avoid the tantrum.[6]

Jesus: Agrees to give her three pink gummy bears to avoid the tantrum.

My Life in Pink:
THE *FROZEN* FILES, PART 1—WHY ELSA RAN

Surely one of the burning questions of our time is, "Can we learn anything from princesses? Or are they completely useless?"

The answer, of course, depends on the princess. If you had the pleasure of meeting my daughter when she was three years old,

---

6 Parents of toddlers will understand that Dad has miscalculated about avoiding the tantrum. We all know what happens to a kid who consumes a bucket of candy.

you might have heard her ask one of her recurring questions about *Frozen*. It was, "Why did Elsa run away?"[7]

"Because she was afraid to hurt the people she loved," I told her again and again.

I can relate. I was alone for many years because fear ruled my life. The backdrop to my solitude might have been religion and Cinderella-type fairy tales, but the truth is that I didn't get into a relationship because lurking behind the highfalutin idea of "meant-to-be" was fear—I was afraid to let myself be vulnerable and get hurt. That's more self-centered than our heroine Elsa, but the fear engine driving my life was the same as hers.

I was in my late twenties when I finally got into a long-term relationship. Even then, the only reason I allowed it to progress was because on some level I sensed it had little chance of succeeding. He was newly divorced and emotionally closed and had even heavier baggage than I did. Yet somehow we came together. After a few years of coupledom, he brought up the possibility of having a baby.

This aroused an even greater fear. I was terrified of becoming a mother. I thought if I had a baby, there was a good chance I'd become depressed again.

Depression. What a colossal waste. If I could time travel, I'd go back to my younger self when I was neck deep in despondency. Then I'd punch myself in the face and say, "Snap out of it."

Sadly, time travel isn't yet within our reach. Also, as anyone who's been in a depression knows, the idea of ejecting depression with a swift blow is just hogwash. If we could snap out of it, we would. But when we're in it, something has gone wrong in our

---

7 "Why did Anna take her glove?" was her other favorite question. This act, which led to all the drama in the movie, vexed Mari for quite a while.

brains. No well-meaning jab-cross-hook combination could have helped me in those days. I finally crawled out because I reached a point where I understood how much depression was costing me. I was wasting my life on sadness.

I got help. I went to therapy, started taking antidepressants and found my way to the surface. In recent years, meditation and exercise have helped me enormously. I still have blue days, but they don't swell into months and years.

Though I was doing better, the shadow of depression kept me afraid. I feared that if I didn't protect myself, depression would return. So when Matt first raised the possibility of having a baby,[8] my first thoughts were, "What if I become a depressed mother? What if I pass my depressive gene on to another generation?"

I know—it's all *fakakt*. I feared. I worried. I avoided life. Depression wasn't coloring my every waking moment, yet it still ruled me. Because buried in the deepest part of me was a very strong desire. I really did want to be a mother. I always had.

Matt and I had a recurring sequence of events. We'd talk about having a baby and then we'd visit his brother, who already had one. His brother and his wife were always in an exhausted fog, which mystified us. "How do people live like this?" we asked each other, after they'd gone upstairs to put the baby to sleep, only to pass out next to her. Then we'd stop talking about having a baby for a while.

Elsa ran away to the mountains because she was afraid and because she fixated on what could go wrong. She only saw the

---

8 My foot-massaging husband, Matt, is the divorced guy I mentioned who had heavier baggage than me. We were both a bit of a fixer-upper. We worked through our shit together. That's my version of a fairy tale.

potential hurt. It was Anna who believed in the potential hope. Anna understood that if Elsa could open up, they'd figure every- thing else out. In order to become a mother, I'd definitely have to channel my inner Anna.[9]

I can't remember the moment when Matt and I finally decided to try to conceive, but I do recall understanding that time was running out. With all my ambivalence, I knew that if I encoun- tered fertility trouble, I might not have the will to persist. So when I reached the age of thirty-five, I stopped taking birth con- trol. It was a leap of faith.

We were very, very lucky. Lucky not to have had fertility prob- lems. And even more lucky to have had a baby.

When I think back on it now, I can hardly believe it. Fear al- most stopped me from having children. That would have truly been a shame. Because becoming a mother was the best thing that ever happened to me.

Mari is far more influenced by the story of Elsa and Anna than by Cinderella's tale. She might like Cindy's dress, but the story of a girl who gets to go to a ball and meet a prince bores her. Whereas the story of two sisters who overcome fear and obstacles fascinates her.

Maybe Mari will approach fear differently than I did. Maybe it won't be a monster to avoid, so much as an icy winter to get through. A girl can wish, can't she?

---

9 Still not sure who Elsa and Anna are? Now we know that you have *definitely* picked up this book by mistake. And yet, you're still reading. I applaud your persistence.

Princess Studies 101:
HOW TO OVERCOME THE FEAR OF PRINCESSES

Behind every feminist mother of a Little Princess lurks a whole set of fears. Will our daughters internalize the idea that appearance is more important than character and spirit? Will they wait around to be saved like the docile Sleepy Trio cream puffs? Will they dedicate valuable time, energy and resources on stuff like snake venom facials[10] and elaborate bridal showers[11] and body-shaping underwear that cuts off your circulation and compresses your organs and causes deadly blood clots?[12] Confronting these fears and resolving them is kind of what this book is about.

The answer to the above questions is that we don't know. The fact that some of our daughters are neck deep in princesses is a relatively new phenomenon because the Disney princess culture evolved recently (which I discuss in chapter 5). There are very few studies that address how the princess culture affects girls. We know that basing self-worth on appearance affects girls badly, but no correlation has been made between girls who love princesses and adolescents or young women who base their self-worth on appearance.

In June 2016, a study that assessed "the princess effect" on 198 preschoolers was published.[13] The study was written about in *Time*, *Fortune*, the *Washington Post* and more than a dozen other places. Headlines about the study included:

---

10 Actually a thing.
11 Also a thing.
12 Someone get me a double vodka.
13 S. M. Coyne et al., "Pretty as a princess: Longitudinal effects of engagement with Disney princesses on gender stereotypes, body esteem, and prosocial behavior in children," *Child Development* 87, no. 6 (2016).

- Are Disney Princesses Hurting Your Daughter's Self-Esteem?

- How Disney Princesses Are Hurting Young Girls

- Are Disney Princess Movies Dangerous for Young Girls?

- Study Suggests Disney Princess Culture Is Harmful for Little Girls

- Could Disney Princesses HARM Your Child?

Not only did the headlines imply that Disney princesses are harmful to little girls, but most of the articles about the study supported the claim.

> The study found that the influence . . . could be damaging to girls—it could make them more susceptible to having bad body esteem and less confidence.
>
> *—Time*

> The effects also extend to body image—those girls that engaged the most with princess culture over time had the lowest body esteem.
>
> *—Fortune*

> A new study has found an association between engagement with Disney princess culture and body image issues in young girls, confirming what many parents have long suspected.
>
> —Slate.com

There was just one problem with all these articles. The study, which said it was the "first study, to our knowledge, to show a long-term effect of Disney Princess engagement during early childhood," never made a connection between girls who liked Disney princesses and diminished self-esteem or body image. Here's what it actually said:

> The second hypothesis was that engagement with Disney Princesses would be related to poor body esteem in girls, due to the perpetuation of the thin ideal by the Disney princess characters. However, princess engagement was not associated with concurrent body esteem for either boys or girls.

This finding was corroborated in another study, which I cite in chapter 4. No one has made the connection yet. I'm not claiming it doesn't exist. But there are no studies that support the theory that little girls who play with, dress up as and love princesses develop lower self-esteem or have higher incidence of negative body image than other girls.

The study did find the following:

- Girls were much more likely than boys to engage with Disney princesses—including playing with princess toys and watching princess media.

- Disney princess engagement was stable across a one-year period, for both boys and girls.

- Princess engagement was "related to higher levels of female gender-stereotypical behavior for both boys and girls." That means that girls who played with princesses were more likely to choose stereotypically "girl" toys such as dolls and tea sets, and more likely to play in "girly" ways like dressing up as opposed to playing sports. The researchers pointed out that stereotypical female behavior "may potentially be problematic," because it might cause girls to feel limited as to what they can do and learn and how they explore the world. And though I'm not dismissing the comment, the results of the study don't suggest that girls who play with princesses will limit themselves. The words "may potentially be problematic" reflect the opinion of the researchers and not the findings, which is why the language is deliberately vague.

- The most interesting finding was that boys who play with princess toys showed "higher levels of female gender-stereotypical behavior" and exhibited more "prosocial" behavior like helping and sharing when studied over the course of one year. The researchers noted the positive effects on boys, as the challenge for many boys is how to negotiate the "hypermasculine messages in the media" that pressure them into burying their sensitive sides.

The study was small in scale and evaluated mostly children from white, middle-class families. It had other limitations as well. All studies do, and the researchers pointed out the limitations freely and honestly, so it's not their fault that the coverage concerning their research was misleading. Studies like these are never definitive but they *are* building blocks. If enough of them are done, conclusions about cause and effect can eventually be made. Yet many newspapers and websites published stories about the study that tried to scare parents of Little Princesses into believing that their tutu-wearing daughters were on the fast train to bubble-brainville.[14]

As a princess-phobe myself, am I saying that we shouldn't fear the princesses? Maybe. The jury is still out on whether princesses

---

14 The *Washington Post* notably wrote about the study in a way that accurately reflected its findings. Its headline was "The Unexpected Way Disney Princesses Affect Little Boys."

matter. We don't know if princess obsession has an adverse effect on girls. It *seems* like it should, but no studies have made the connection. The long-term research that could address this question—which must include studies of teenagers and adult women who identify as having been princess obsessed as children and evaluate whether they have lower self-esteem or higher incidence of depression or even have a greater likelihood of being bubbleheads—hasn't been done yet. One 2011 study suggests that at least some of these princess-obsessed girls become tomboys in adolescence—a statistic that might comfort mothers like me—but notes the lack of longitudinal data that could predict anything conclusive.[15] Until there is more data, all we really have is our best guess about whether the pink proclivity is problematic.

Dr. Sarah M. Coyne, the lead researcher of the 2016 study, offered parents the advice to "have your kids involved in all sorts of activities, and just have princesses be one of many, many things that they like to do and engage with."

Coyne would also like to conduct future research that would follow the study's children into middle school to see how the princess culture influences them over time. We should definitely consider Dr. Coyne's sensible advice. There's lots of other things parents of Little Princesses can do that might offset the chances that their daughters will have low self-esteem. But for now at least, let's let go of the fear. It didn't help Elsa, and it's surely not helping our daughters.

---

15 May Ling Halim et al., "From pink frilly dresses to 'one of the boys': A social-cognitive analysis of gender identity development and gender bias," *Social and Personality Psychology Compass* 5, issue 11 (2011).

Opposite of Serious:
THE FEMTASTIC GODMOTHER
AND *SLEEPING BEAUTY*

Disney may have botched the new Cinderella, *but that's no reason for those of us with princess-obsessed daughters to despair. Knowing Disney, they'll eventually produce future versions of the princess stories. Since I'm such a magnanimous gal, I've decided to help them out. I've appointed a feminist fairy godmother to brainstorm how to make the films worthy of our Little Princesses, and even relevant to actual living people. Here she is:*

Isn't she fabulous? Don't you wish she was *your* fairy godmother? I think she might be available for birthday parties, so if you can't rent an "Elsa" or an "Ariel," do keep her in mind.

Let's see how she uses her bippity-boppity-boo magic to update *Sleeping Beauty* and make the main characters just a little bit more relatable to us modern gals.

✦ ✦ ✦

Old *Sleeping Beauty*: Once upon a time, two kings promised that their baby children would marry each other to unite the two kingdoms.

Why do people want more stuff when they already have enough stuff?

Femtastic *Sleeping Beauty*: Once upon a time, two queens told their two kings to ease up on the brandy and to stop pretending that their newborn children were plastic pawns on a child's board game.

◆ ◆ ◆

Old *Sleeping Beauty*: Once upon a time, a sorceress named Maleficent was enraged that she hadn't been invited to a party celebrating the birth of a baby.

Maybe the e-vite went into her spam?

Femtastic *Sleeping Beauty*: Once upon a time, a powerful woman was supposed to go to a baby shower, but when the party was canceled she couldn't believe her luck because she got to stay home and binge watch *Game of Thrones* instead.

✦ ✦ ✦

Old *Sleeping Beauty*: Once upon a time, Maleficent cast a spell on Aurora so that when she turned sixteen, she'd prick her finger on a spinning wheel and drop dead.

Femtastic *Sleeping Beauty*: Once upon a time, Maleficent cast a spell on Aurora so that when she turned sixteen, she'd learn about birth control and then wouldn't have to drop out of school because she'd gotten pregnant in the rented limo on junior prom night.

✦ ✦ ✦

Old *Sleeping Beauty*: Once upon a time, Princess Aurora and Prince Phillip—who believed they were perfect strangers—met in the forest, danced together and fell in love.

Femtastic *Sleeping Beauty*: Once upon a time, Princess Aurora and Prince Phillip met in the forest and danced together, but then discovered that their fathers knew each other and, worse, that they actually *wanted* them to marry one another. They were completely creeped out and agreed never to see each other again.

✦ ✦ ✦

Old *Sleeping Beauty*: Once upon a time, Prince Phillip kissed Princess Aurora, who was fast asleep at the time.

That story always gives me the willies.

Femtastic *Sleeping Beauty*: Once upon a time, Prince Phillip read that one in five American women say they were sexually assaulted in college, including many instances of women being assaulted while they were passed out. So he took the It's On Us pledge, recognizing that nonconsensual sex is sexual assault. And they all lived happily ever after.

✦ ✦ ✦

Interesting Little Princess Fact #2

I was going to write a Disney princess reality show transcript where all the princesses have to live in a castle together and bitch at each other, but then discovered that *Saturday Night Live* already did that.

✦ ✦ ✦

Little Princess Pie

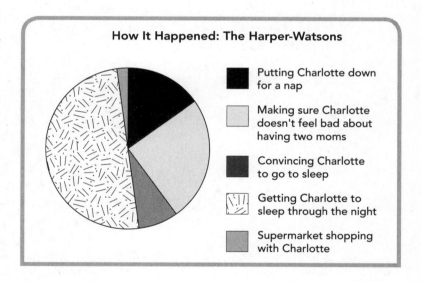

How It Happened: The Harper-Watsons

- Putting Charlotte down for a nap
- Making sure Charlotte doesn't feel bad about having two moms
- Convincing Charlotte to go to sleep
- Getting Charlotte to sleep through the night
- Supermarket shopping with Charlotte

In our second Little Princess case study, Charlotte recently asked her moms, "Where's my daddy?"

The two women, who were both suffering from extreme exhaustion due to Charlotte's unfortunate resistance to sleep, quickly fell into a guilt-ridden black hole. For an entire month Charlotte's mothers bought her nothing but tutus and sparkly shoes.

By the time the Harper-Watsons emerged from their magenta matrix, it was too late. Charlotte was a Little Princess.

Though sleep deprivation is still their greatest challenge, the mothers are also prone to purchasing princess merchandise in supermarket checkout lines, where Charlotte likes to grab packs of gum and throw them at other shoppers. A Rapunzel Pez dispenser or a few Glitzi Globes princess Surprise Eggs will usually get them all to the minivan in one piece.

Chapter 3

MIRROR, MIRROR, ON THE WALL, WHO'S THE CONTROL-FREAKIEST OF THEM ALL?

My Life in Pink:
ONCE UPON A VERY IRRITATING BOOK

When Mari was born, our house was princess-free. Like all good feminists, I kept our home clear of anything that looked or smelled remotely pink. We didn't even eat cupcakes.[1]

That didn't change with Color Week at Mari's preschool. Our gender-neutral sanctum was infiltrated one month before she started preschool when well-meaning relatives[2] sent her a present for her second birthday. It was a book—one of those press-the-buttons-on-the-side books that plays tinny, familiar songs like "If You're Happy and You Know It" and "The More We Get Together." Adorable, right? But the book cover was bubblegum pink, it was called *Once Upon a Song* and there were three Disney princesses on

---

1 Because I can't bake.
2 It was my in-laws.

the cover decked out in sparkly satin dresses. This was Mari's first princess book. It was Mari's first princess anything.

Blissfully ignorant as we were, with no idea where our lives were headed, the book didn't alarm me. I saw it as an isolated item. A fragment of some strange, regressive culture awash in our sea of sensible children's books choices.

It's just one book, I told myself. *Besides, what am I going to do? Throw away a present sent by well-meaning relatives?*[3]

I didn't like it, though. The musical aspect was sweet, yet it seemed like a thinly disguised Disney advertisement. The book was dull and uninspiring, just like the Sleepy Trio themselves. Mari loved it instantly, however. I mean she *loved* it—like, all the other books felt abandoned and sank into depression. *Goodnight Moon* was especially needy, bingeing on gourmet pretzels and tortilla chips.

"Read it again," she'd say, as soon as we'd finished reading *Once Upon a Song.*

"Again," she'd repeat, once we'd read it a second time.

"Again."

Well, anyone who's ever met a toddler knows where this is going. "Toddler" and "Repetition" are a little like Thing One and Thing Two—they always go together and they destroy your house.

Before we knew what was happening, *Once Upon a Song* had insinuated itself into our daily lives. Instead of enjoying *The Foot Book* and *If You Give a Pig a Pancake* and the Sandra Boynton oeuvre, I was instead forced to look at this weird, plotless princess fest.

What can I do? I asked myself again. *We're stuck with it.*

---

3 If you recall, we're talking about my in-laws. Rejecting their gift would be like lighting up a cigarette while filling the tank with super unleaded. Unadvisable.

I had another issue with the book. Like many Disney products that plug the princesses, *Once Upon a Song* showcased the white ones. Ariel, Aurora, Snow White and Cinderella each get a page, and Tiana also appears, but I suspect it's because the book was published a year after *The Princess and the Frog*—Tiana's flick—was released. Pocahontas and Mulan are left out. In general, the most marketed princesses are the white ones, with the exception of Jasmine.

So not only was this book introducing nutty, rail-thin feminine images to my daughter, it was also exposing her to a narrow and limited view of the world, one that excluded people of color. Even worse, the songs were played in keys that are physically impossible for a grown woman to sing. Okay, that's not worse. But if you ever had the misfortune of hearing me sing along to one of those songs, you might have mistaken me for an old computer attempting a dial-up Internet connection.[4]

In short, *Once Upon a Song* was ruining our lives!

Too dramatic? How about this?

Once Upon a Song was annoying! It was a book for toddler dummies! It was hindering my efforts to raise my daughter in a conscious and progressive and thoughtful way. It sucked!

Which is why I changed my mind. There *was* something I could do about it, I decided. I could get rid of it.

(Cue villainous "dun dun duuuun" music.)

I started to plot against *Once Upon a Song*. Like the evil queen in Snow White, I devised ways to get the book out of our lives. Initially I tried to hide it. I slipped it in a drawer under the radio/CD player, which I'm not at all embarrassed that we technophobes still possessed. If Mari didn't see the book lying around,

---

4 Anyone? How old are you people anyway?

I reasoned, she'd forget about it. We kept our appliance manuals in this drawer, so I figured it would be safe there.

Unbeknownst to me, however, Cai had been planting rummy tiles around the house, pretending they were secret cameras.[5] He was going through a secret agent phase and while planting one of these "cameras" in the drawer, he found the book. He was very proud of himself when he returned it to his little sister. What a hero.

I came up with a new cunning plan. I would wait for Mari to go to preschool and then dispose of the book. When she came home, I'd pretend it was lost. After a few days, surely it would be forgotten. How much does a two-year-old really understand anyway? Weeks after she turned two, Mari was still walking around saying, "It was my birthday yesterday."

I realize that this all sounds bonkers. You try singing "Beautiful Dreamer" ninety-three times in a row, and then judge me.

One morning I dropped Mari off at her program and returned home. The book was easy to find since, in those days, it really *was* the only pink item around. If I had to find it today, it would be like finding a pink needle in a pink haystack in a pink barn in a pink fifth dimension.

I had the book in hand and headed for the door. At the threshold, I spotted Mari's baby leather shoes. They were bright green with pictures of smiling turtles on them. Mari wore proper shoes by then, but once in a while she still liked to wear the soft turtle shoes, just for fun. This was something that characterized her play—she loved to take off clothes and put on clothes and hats and jewelry and anything else she found lying around. She made my skirts into dresses and my shirts into shawls and veils.

---

5 I guess this was known to me on some level, as there were suddenly rummy tiles everywhere.

Though she was only two years old, she already liked shopping and getting new items of clothing more than toys.

This love for clothing and accessories didn't come from me. I actively hate shopping and I'll wear the same outfit five days in a row, as long as it doesn't smell. Mari hadn't learned dress-up from Cai, either, for whom clothing is a functional means not to be naked. Mari's clothing play also preceded her attending pre-school and her interactions with other kids. This is something that came from inside her.

I looked at the book I was about to banish from our home. Mari loved it and I was throwing it away. What the hell was I doing? I really *had* become the evil queen. I may not have needed to be the fairest in the land, but I was still trying to manipulate the world according to my wishes rather than accept its ebb and flow.

Mari wasn't me. I didn't like the book, but she did. Why couldn't I accept that? What was I so afraid of?

Those of us who dislike the princess culture are just trying to do what's best for our girls. We want them to have fulfilling lives and not be held back by limiting perceptions about what it is to be female. Even I had to admit that it was a stretch to associate this book with that aspiration. We could read the book a thousand more times—and probably did—yet I was still Mari's mother. She wasn't alone and lost in the woods with a sinister wolf telling her she was bad at math.

Mari has influences on her life that are not me, and they're all worthy and offer her something enriching. Along with *Once Upon a Song*, Matt's parents have sent her some of her subsequent favorite books, like *Hippo Has a Hat* and *The Rhyming Rabbit*.

Matt is a loving and sensitive father and Cai is a terrific and engaging older brother. My parents and family shower my kids with love, attention and thoughtfulness. They may not buy her exactly what I would purchase or say the things I would, but everyone is playing a positive role in Mari's life. Mari is playing an important role too—expressing love and enthusiasm for the things she likes. If I try to put up walls between her and her passions rather than encouraging them, that makes me kind of a jerk. Not to mention a crummy mother.

I put the book back on the coffee table where Mari would spot it as soon as she came home.

It's funny now to think back on that episode. Color Week would soon change our lives forever. If I had thrown out the book only to have Mari become obsessed with pink and princesses anyway, I would have felt like a complete idiot.

A few weeks later, a Frog and Toad anthology became the book Mari wanted to read over and over again. For a while, *Carla's Sandwich* was read daily. It was written by a woman I know named Debbie Herman and it's about how being different is hard at first, but ultimately rewarding and earns the respect of others.

We still read *Once Upon a Song* sometimes. About six months after we received the book, the batteries ran out and we couldn't listen to the tunes anymore. One afternoon I dropped Mari off at school and came home. I took the book and snuck it out of the house. Then I went to an electronics store and had the tiny batteries replaced, so we could read it again and again and again.

Opposite of Serious

*When you have a princess-obsessed daughter, Christmas/Hanukkah/
Eid is a hazardous time. No matter what you tell well-meaning relatives about the kinds of gifts your child would like, they know the truth. And how could they not? Your princess advertises it daily with her tiara and blinding pink neon tights.*

Unlike you, many of these relatives are unreconstructed lovers of princesses. Others have "good intentions," which means they understand that you're trying not to raise a passive, marriage-obsessed cream puff, and they believe they've followed the spirit of your instructions with their holiday offering. Either way, you're screwed. During the holiday season, your house is about to get even pinker.

Holiday Gifts for Little Princesses

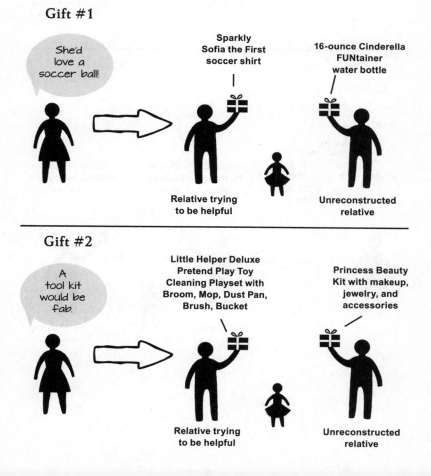

Gift #3

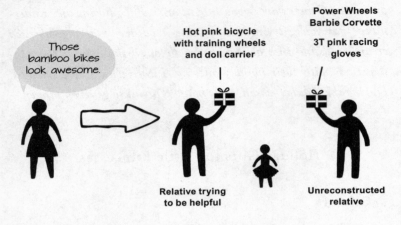

Gift #4

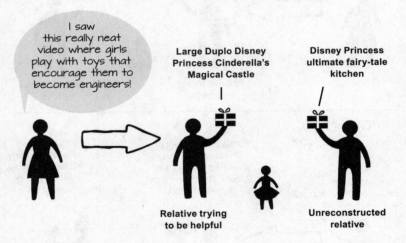

Interesting Little Princess Fact #3

Mari's older brother, Cai, likes *Frozen* even though he says he doesn't. If we turn the film on for Mari, he'll open a book and pretend to read it as he secretly watches the movie.

✦ ✦ ✦

My Life in Pink:
CAULIFLOWER GODDESSES, STICKER CHARTS AND JANET JACKSON

So what was all that about anyway? I mean the ballad of *Once Upon a Song*, in which a mother tries to throw away a book she doesn't like even though her daughter loves it.

It's about the hardest thing you'll ever have to do as a parent: cleaning up vomit from the crevices of a toddler bed frame at three a.m.

Oh, wait, sorry. That's the second hardest thing. The hardest thing you'll ever have to do as a parent is give up control.

I'm not the smartest person, but I am a forty-five-year-old woman. This means that, at the very least, I've gained more wisdom than my children, who—without trying to insult them—have so little wisdom that they have done the following:

1. Found gum under a table at the shopping mall and then popped it into their mouth.

2. Insisted they did not need socks on an arctic, record-breaking-snowfall day.

3. Gotten their tooth stuck in the pull tab of a zipper on a slipper that someone was *wearing at the time.*

4. Insisted they *did* need socks on a scorching day when Mother Nature apparently decided that a sauna would be nice.

I could go on, but that's just the kind of thing that happens when you're, like, two or four or even six years old. You have no idea what you're doing most of the time, which is why parents aren't expendable. If kids were born sensible, they'd be telling us to stop binge watching *Game of Thrones* and get some sleep.

So I find myself advising my children all the time.

"Stop getting so worked up about candy," I might say, or, "If you would just get dressed now, I wouldn't turn into a kraken when it's time to leave the house," or, "FOR GOD'S SAKE, SPIT OUT THAT GUM!"

And do you know what's really vexing? They won't listen to me. Isn't that sad? Here I am with so much knowledge they could learn from, and they won't *listen*.

When Cai was six, he would regularly lie to his friends. This would have alarmed me, except that his friends did the same thing. They lied about seeing *Star Wars*, about beating a grandmaster at chess, about owning games and devices and about all kinds of random and weird stuff.[6] I guess that's just what first grade boys do. They aren't the most logical people. They're little monkeys, really. They used to play a game where they punched each other in the penis.

But behind the lying I feared something sinister happening—that the seeds of a false self were being planted in my son. That

---

6 One kid claimed to be so strong that he punched a windshield and shattered it with his bare six-year-old hand. And everyone in the class believed him.

he was learning he wasn't good enough and had to embellish and lie to be accepted. I tried to talk to him about it. "If people are impressed by stupid things like who owns a Wii," I told him, "then those people aren't worth your time. You are terrific just as you are."

Fabulous stuff, right? Yet Cai ignored me. He even said, "I'm not listening to you. I know what I'm doing."

This wasn't an isolated incident. Whenever I tried to tell Cai something I believed was important, he tuned me out. Like with the whole "eating" thing. Cai was one of those white-food kids for whom bread, pasta and yogurt were nourishment, while anything that even suggested vitamin C was diabolical.

"Just try one tiny bite of carrot," I'd say. This kind of suggestion was always followed by about five minutes of excruciating lunacy. Cai would look miserably at his plate, his eyes lifeless as if we'd subjected him to ten hours of uninterrupted bridal shower games. He was so convincing in his suffering that I'd start to resent the existence of vegetables myself.

Like so many mamas, the subject of food occupied me.

What if eating poorly gives him scurvy? I'd think. *What if he doesn't get into college because of all that peanut butter? What if his refusal to take a bite of quinoa brings on the Apocalypse?*[7]

I constantly tried to help him. I'd cut up apples in the shape of stars, make a smiley face out of peas and corn, compose operettas about avocado and build pagan altars to the cruciferous goddesses of cauliflower. Nothing worked. In fact, the more I tried, the more Cai refused to eat anything healthy.

Why was he being such a bonehead?

---

7 We're Jewish, so we'd really be screwed.

Let's fast-forward. Just before he turned four, the vitamin-averse Cai was joined by a baby sister. Her name was Mari, and about a year and a half later she started to bite. Other people, I mean.

I mentioned this—before she became a Little Princess, Mari was a Little Biter. At the time, this made me feel terrible. Kids were getting hurt because of my daughter. Other parents were angry. One of them was shaming me and Mari and trying to get her kicked out of preschool. I dreaded picking her up every day at her preschool program and facing the judgment of others.

And as with Cai and food, I did everything I could to help Mari correct her behavior. I consulted with other parents and read articles and prescriptive advice on the subject. We spoke with parents who had used sticker charts and positive reinforcement, a few that had given time-outs and one couple who had put their daughter in a cold shower whenever she bit.

Readers of chapter 2 might recall that in the end, we decided to make a "gentle hands" sticker chart. I wish I could say that I never yelled at Mari for biting, but I did. There were times when after the preschool pickup, confronted by the bite marks on another child's skin, I yelled at her in the car on the way home.

"Stop biting!" I'd yell. "It's not okay!"

Imagine being a two-year-old trapped in a car with a yelling parent. My poor daughter. This was a parenting fail too big to make a joke about. I cringe remembering those afternoons.

And of course all of my focus in those days was misguided and a sad waste of time. If I'd been listening closely, I would have discovered something important—something we eventually came to understand after the drama had passed. All the parents we consulted said the exact same thing. No matter what method they'd used, the biting stopped around the time the child turned three.

I wasn't listening, because I was too busy making sticker charts to solve a problem that needed fixing. Yet ask anyone who has worked with preschoolers—toddlers stop biting when the biting stage passes. Not because you've convinced your two-year-old that filling a page with smiley faces is more compelling than the urge to chomp another kid. Toddler minds aren't really thinking things through. They're *really* little monkeys.

Some problems don't have a quick fix or any fix at all. That's a very hard truth to accept, especially as a parent. And we all know that the problems get much worse than toddler aggression.

All of this—my reaction to *Once Upon a Song*, the Cai Food Wars and the Bad Days of Reality Biting—is really about the same thing. My need to control.

I know I'm not the only one out there with this issue. Look at King Triton. He destroyed Ariel's collection of human doodads in her grotto. Come to think of it, he was a much bigger dick-head than me. You see how princess movies always make us feel better?

Still, two wrong parents don't make a right. It took me a while to figure out that when Cai shut down on me, he wasn't reacting to the carrots or my inept strategies to make asparagus look like a stick man. He was reacting to my need to control him.

Control. It's at once a hit 1986 Janet Jackson song and one of our deepest needs. As I wrote this book, control issues cropped up too many times to count. No matter how much I try to be self-aware, the urge to mold the earth according to my design always seems to creep back into my subconscious.

So what's a mother to do?

During Mari's "biting season" I met with her teacher a few times. During one of those meetings she said, "I think Mari bites because she's one of the smallest in the group. She does it when she feels powerless and out of control."

Tears welled in my eyes when she said that. I knew just how my daughter felt. Feeling small and vulnerable in the world is no fun at all. Having no control stinks. And when the powerlessness extends to your kids, it seems unbearable. How can it be that I created life and now have so little say in what happens to that life? Who died and made me not boss?

I'm not the boss. I'm just the mother. I can do my best to teach and protect and comfort. But I can't control everything.

Isn't it funny how we keep trying anyway? We try to control their sleep and their eating and their pooping. As they grow older, the list of things we want to manipulate just grows and grows. We hang on for dear life. And then our kids do whatever they want. They don't listen.

As it happened, Mari stopped biting a little before schedule—a few months shy of turning three. Who knows? Maybe the sticker chart helped after all.

Or maybe it was something else I did.

I can't prove it but I do think it had an effect—if not on the biting, then at least on repairing my connection with my daughter after I'd yelled at her for something she couldn't help. It's one of those things that I will try to do again and again, at least when I don't suffer from the stress-induced amnesia that makes us forget our wisdom.

I surrendered to the fact that I had no control.

I told myself, again and again, "I accept that I can't control this." I told it to myself like a mantra until I believed it, until I could pick Mari up at preschool without that rigid expectation that things had to be a certain way, and I could accept her the way she was and drive home with love in my heart rather than anger and criticism and rejection.

Maybe Mari absorbed my surrender and on some level started to accept the same thing for herself.

I'm not saying that I'll never make another chart—our sticker purchases have probably bought at least one sticker magnate a googly-eyed yacht. I'm a parent, after all, and teaching my kids right from wrong is part of the job description. I just know that when my need to control overshadows my capacity to love, I lose. And when I surrender to what *is* instead of holding on to how I want life to be, everyone I love wins.

Princess Studies 101:
CONTROLLING PARENTS MIGHT BE A LITTLE WORSE THAN PRINCESSES AND FAIRY-TALE NARRATIVES

Trying not to control your kids is like trying to get that thirty minutes of aerobic exercise in every day. You know it's what you're supposed to do, yet you keep falling short.

For me, and I imagine for other parents, the first time I faced my ugliest tendencies to try to control my children was when they were toddlers. The urge to put an end to that humiliating public tantrum is overwhelming. Sadly, so are the odds against your succeeding.

Psychologists say that tantrums occur when children can't regulate their emotions. That may be true, but perhaps meltdowns are also built into the behavior of young children in order to teach us parents a lesson about giving in to the chaos. Because if you can do it—if you can let go of your need to control your child in the supermarket when she is going bananas because you haven't put the box of multicolored cereal in your shopping cart and people are staring and your cart is way too full to bail and retreat to the parking lot and you seriously wonder why anyone even has children in an age of available birth control—if you can actually accept what's happening at that moment, then maybe you can do parenthood in general. Maybe the next twenty years of your life will be challenging rather than unbearable, enriching rather than a source of constant misery. But what do I know? I don't even have children in the double digits yet.

I can sense that controlling my kids is bad, however. It *feels* bad when I'm doing it. I'm not talking about teaching them how to behave—I'm referring to the times when I'm trying to control my kids with manipulation, through guilt, by withholding affection and by making decisions for them.

Am I right? Is trying to control kids really such a bad thing?

In 2014, a psychology professor surveyed 297 college students and found a link between inappropriate levels of parental control and the negative well-being of the young adults. People with controlling parents were more likely to be depressed, feel dissatisfied with life and have lower levels of perceived competence—meaning they didn't believe in their own abilities.[8]

Other studies support the idea that controlling kids is bad: A 2015 University College London study found that adults who were psychologically controlled by their parents were more likely

---

8 H. H. Schiffrin et al., "Helping or hovering? The effects of helicopter parenting on college students' well-being," *Journal of Child and Family Studies* 23, no. 3 (2014).

to have poor mental health and were less satisfied and happy.[9] A 2012 study from the University of New Hampshire found that authoritarian parents were more likely to raise disrespectful and delinquent kids.[10] And a 2014 University of Virginia study found that adults who were psychologically controlled during their teenage years might have a harder time handling disagreements as adults and also have difficulty developing close relationships.[11]

I could go on, but the point is that I couldn't find one single study that suggested that controlling your kids was a good thing.

Which makes the confusion of how to be a decent parent all the more vexing. What are we meant to do, exactly? If our kids are clay, are we the potter's wheel or the potter? If we're the latter, are we supposed to shape them or simply throw them at the pottery wheel and look on admiringly as they somehow become earthen bowls? What I mean is, when should we hold on and when do we let go? Were bullies controlled too much or too little? Did adults who cheat elderly people out of their savings have parents who were too permissive or too manipulative? Are reality TV villains the result of coddling parents or parents who forced them to play in playgrounds made of wooden planks with rusty nails?

Gosh, I have no idea, and so sorry if you were looking for

---

9 M. Stafford et al., "Parent–child relationships and offspring's positive mental wellbeing from adolescence to early older age." *Journal of Positive Psychology* 11, no. 3 (2015).

10 R. Trinkner et al., "Don't trust anyone over 30: Parental legitimacy as a mediator between parenting style and changes in delinquent behavior over time," *Journal of Adolescence* 35, no. 1 (2012).

11 B. A. Oudekerk et al., "The cascading development of autonomy and relatedness from adolescence to adulthood," *Child Development* 86, no. 2 (2014).

answers to that question in this book about Little Princesses. I'll just say that every kid is different. Their needs—including how many rules are best for them and how much freedom is ideal—change over time. Getting it wrong sometimes is simply part of parenting.

Also, parental instinct should be honored more than the advice of others. By "others" I include judgmental friends, well-meaning relatives, articles and books about parenting and, of course, that bastion of incessant criticism, the Internet. When it comes to your kids, you can usually trust yourself.

Opposite of Serious

Confused about which parenting style works best for you? Who could blame you? Why do we even need a "parenting style"? Isn't it enough that we have to make dinner every night?

Free-Range vs. Helicopter Parenting: Get the Facts

1. *What are Free-Range and Helicopter parenting?*
Free-Range and Helicopter parenting are two different and opposing parenting styles that illustrate what happens to a flourishing postindustrial society with excess leisure time. This also explains why *The Bachelor* is in its twenty-first season.

2. *Which parenting style is dominant in America?*
The wrong one. Everyone knows that Europeans raise their children better than American parents do. So do Asian parents,

African parents and Australian parents. All parents every-where, so long as they are not you.

3. *How can . . .*

Wait. I forgot. Antarctic parents are also superior to American parents. So are Great Hornbill parents.

4. *How can you be a parent who is involved but not smothering?*

Just remember to have your children operate heavy machinery after you tie their shoelaces for them and decorate their dorm room.

5. *Why do people judge Helicopter moms?*

Judging women for their choices is a national pastime.

6. *What should a Helicopter mom say to someone who tells her that her parenting style is just a form of narcissism?*

Say, "If loving my kid is wrong, I don't want to be right." Either that or "Hover off."

7. *Are people who are struggling to make ends meet more likely to be Helicopter parents or Free-Range parents?*

They are the very parents most likely to never dwell on the subject.

8. *I'm trying to get up the courage to go Free Range. What should I do now?*

The first thing you need to do is have a child. Then read up on statistics about how many children are injured or killed in ways that are entirely unrelated to abductions. Shootings, drownings, ingesting poisonous substances—really, it's endless! Immerse yourself in the morbid data and understand that there are so many different and unexpected ways it could happen. Now relax and set your child free.

9. *Which type of parenting style will increase my child's chances of going to a good college?*
The kind where you earn enough money to pay $29,000 in annual tuition.

10. *Why has the founder of Free-Range Kids been called "America's Worst Mom"?*
See No. 5.

11. *Why are Free-Range parents getting arrested?*
That's a common misconception. It's actually the children who are getting arrested.[12]

12. *Isn't it dangerous to leave a child unattended?*
It depends if your child is a sensible, mature person or an erratic toddler who licks the surfaces in public toilets and thinks she can fly.

---

12 In April 2015, Child Protective Services took two children, aged six and ten, into custody as they walked home from a park two and a half blocks away from their home and kept them for three hours without notifying their parents. Their parents, who advocate Free-Range parenting, were accused of neglect by CPS for allowing their kids to walk home alone. If you let your kids walk home alone, that's okay. If you don't, that's also okay. But let's agree that CPS was thoroughly out of line for detaining those poor kids.

13. *How do I know if I'm a Free-Range or Helicopter parent?*
You are neither. Most people are not sufficiently ideologically committed to one style or the other to make a conscious, informed decision. Instead, they change their parenting approach according to the most recent persuasive article they've read on the subject.

14. *How will that inconsistency affect my children?*
Very badly. Most experts agree that consistency is the most important factor in raising emotionally healthy children.

15. *Oh, dear!*
Don't worry. Actually, scratch that. Worry.

Opposite of Serious

The desire to control our children begins even before they're born. Once they're babies, however, we go into overdrive. That's why people make pointless baby stuff we don't need and then try to sell it to us. When I read an article about a new trend of baby bodysuits with magnetic parts and attachments designed to track things like skin temperature and movement and oxygen levels, I was appalled but hardly surprised. This is my satirical take on the "wired" baby products.

The Unmonitored Baby Is Not Worth Having

In case the current crop of wired onesies isn't enough, a few more have recently appeared on the market.

Sleep-O

Sleep-O is a bodysuit for baby that transmits reams of data straight to your iPhone. You will immediately know if baby has turned over, drooled or abruptly started to speak like Henry Kissinger. Sleep-O requires a Bluetooth wireless base station to be plugged in inside the baby's room and comes with a magnetically charged cuddly toy to be placed in the crib with baby.

Poop-O

Poop-O takes the guesswork out of assessing the physical presence of fecal matter. By attaching a wireless sensor to the inside of your baby's diaper, Poop-O will identify, quantify and correctly gauge the consistency of all bowel movements. Poop-O sends automatic text notifications to your smartphone as well as messages to your Gmail and Facebook accounts. An Instagram image and "Pin It" option is currently in beta mode. Poop-O is easily cleaned using a battery-operated UV sterilizer.

Drink-O

Drink-O is a BPA-free plastic bottle with a built-in filter system that purifies water. Best of all, Drink-O has a special flavor-infusing chamber that adds a dose of cherry-enhanced glucose powder if sensors indicate baby isn't drinking. Your baby will never be dehydrated with this sleek, stylish bottle that provides maximum water tastiness for the littlest drinkers.

Feed-O

Feed-O solves the age-old problem of timing your baby's first solid feed. This simple intra-abdominal pressure-monitoring device will pinpoint exactly when your baby is ready to ingest solid foods. You will never again have to prepare and feed mashed pear or cereal to a baby whose digestive system is a few weeks too young to process complex carbohydrates. Mildly annoying gas is a thing of the analog past with Feed-O.

Cry-O

A smartphone-enabled mobile headset is now available and can determine with 97 percent accuracy that your baby is crying. With a headset inspired by Winnie the Pooh and a rainbow-colored strap that fits most babies, Cry-O projects a matrix of custom screenshots to your baby's visual arena at the onset of wails. According to initial research, most babies will eventually associate the barrage of images with the idea that someone is coming to comfort them.

Read-O

Fill in your baby's data, strap on the electrodes and voilà! The Read-O app will choose baby books based on your baby's likely preferences. This app connects directly to your Amazon account and purchases the books without any inconvenience to parents. Upgrade to Read-O Pro, and the app will also read to your baby. Upgrade to Read-O Pro Plus and the app will read to your baby in the voice of Henry Kissinger.

Little Princess Pie

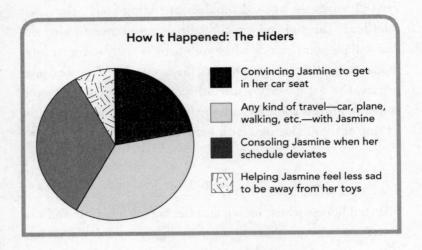

Sometimes the Hiders erroneously believe that if they hadn't named their daughter Jasmine, she might have turned out differently. Maybe she would be able to go with the flow more. Perhaps she would have been able to skip a nap without making everyone in the family bitterly regret going on a road trip more than thirty minutes away from their home. Or the family might have been able to visit Florida without such dire consequences.

But a Little Princess by any other name would be as high maintenance. Jasmine would have resisted any kind of travel even if she'd been named Amelia or Sally. And since Jasmine would strenuously like to stay home all the time, the only way to reassure her that everything is right with the world when she *does* leave the house is to make sure she has all her princess MagiClip dolls with her. Also her princess baby dolls. And the princess plush dolls. Finally, no trip outside the threshold of Jasmine's home is ever possible without her princess doll cake toppers.

Chapter 4

CONGRATULATIONS!
IT'S A *BEAUTIFUL*!

My Life in Pink:
BEAUTY SCHOOL DROPOUT

She's beautiful!

If I had a nickel for every time someone told me that about Mari, I'd have a distressing quantity of nickels.

And if I had a nickel for every time someone told me, *She's smart!* I'd still be cursing the day they invented princess Pull-Ups.[1]

When you have an adorable little girl who wears pink, people instantly respond to her. They compliment her and fuss over her and generally give her more attention than she gets when she wears, say, a T-shirt with an image of a duck on it. Even a really cute, fuzzy duck.

---

1 The exorbitant cost of princess Pull-Ups is a leading cause of divorce, followed by communications problems and infrequent sex. And yet no one seems to care.

When you have an adorable girl who wears pink *and* princessy clothing, the attention she receives swells to comic proportions. As an added bonus, she'll often get called "Princess."

A chicken-and-egg-inclined parent might start asking herself which came first. Did my daughter love pink and the attention followed? Or did all that attention make my daughter love pink?

I'll never know the answer to this question. I know the answer to this one, though: What happens to a girl who derives her confidence from her appearance?

Answer: Her self-esteem nosedives around adolescence when her body starts to become the focal point of her feelings of self-worth. We all know why this happens. Our society has a very specific concept of the female beauty ideal, and absolutely no one looks like that ideal except a woman named Valeria Lukyanova, who claims to subsist on air and water and calls herself "the Human Barbie."

It's funny because women have made such enormous leaps and yet we can't shake the worship of "pretty."[2] In fact, the pressures on women and girls seem to have gotten only more entrenched in the last decade. Girls feel the need to look beautiful at ever younger ages, and at the other end of the age spectrum women are expected to look young and sexy after they turn forty and fifty and sixty and did you see Christie Brinkley rocking the red carpet at Barbie's fifty-fifth birthday party? She was sixty but kind of looked thirty and it was all really weird especially since it was a birthday party for Barbie who was in her midfifties yet her body was still as unrealistic as ever unless you happened to be BFFs with Valeria Lukyanova.[3]

---

2 It's not really funny.
3 In which case you'd definitely feel fat and ugly all the time.

So what's a mother to do? How do I teach a little girl who gets love and attention for being beautiful that beauty is transient and a flimsy basis for self-worth?

Don't worry. I got this. I've researched it thoroughly and here's what I'm doing:

1. I never say "I look fat" or "I look skinny" in front of my daughter or call attention to my weight in general.

2. I never focus on how I'm aging.

3. If I tell Mari she's beautiful, I say, "You're beautiful on the inside and out."

4. I exercise with the goal of being healthy and not with the intent to stay youthful and avoid weight gain.

5. I don't spend excessive amounts of money on beauty products or clothing items designed to make me look slimmer or sexier.

6. Neither do I expend inappropriate energy on trying to look youthful.

7. Mari will not be exposed to beauty or cosmetic products of any kind.

8. I point out how media manipulates us into believing in an unobtainable beauty ideal.

Isn't that a great list? Aren't I fantastic? Most of you can just go ahead and skip to the next chapter, basking in the glow of my breathtaking fabulousness.

Wait—you're still reading? I suppose that means that you're not buying it. And for you, readers who know better, here's the honest list of what I do:

1. After I had a stomach flu and didn't eat for three days, I looked in the mirror and announced, "Look how skinny I look!" Once, when I was eating, I said, "I'd better stop before I get fat," and only afterward remembered there were impressionable children seated at the table. I used to say to Cai, "If you eat you grow taller, but when I eat I just grow this way," while pointing to my stomach. My observations about my fluctuating bloat are far too numerous to mention.

2. Most of my wrinkles actually don't bother me—at least not yet—but I'm consistently surprised by my sagging jowls. It's like I focus all my aging anxiety on these two slumping spodges on my face.[4] Recently I had one of those moments when I wasn't prepared to see my reflection so I saw the unfiltered truth—and really saw how I looked. My sags bothered me in a deep, unfamiliar way. Realizing I had lost all perspective (by forgetting there are children in the world living in war zones, for example), I tried something new: I told my sags that I loved them (which admittedly still doesn't help any of those children).

3. I tell Mari she's beautiful all the time. Sometimes I say, "You're smart and beautiful and it's more important to be smart." Of course that's true, but smart can also be a shaky basis for self-esteem so I consider this a parenting fail. Self-esteem has to come from somewhere else, from a place that can't be judged or evaluated by external forces.

4. I certainly do yoga to stay mentally healthy. Yet I'd be lying through my teeth if I said I didn't like how it affects my body. I saw stomach tone for the first time ever at age forty-three. That made me very happy.

---

4 "Spodges" is not a word, but shouldn't we make it one?

5. I've expended significant amounts of time, not to mention monetary investment, on hair care products—all in the hopes of preventing my hair from resembling transparent vermicelli rice noodles. If you knew how much money I've spent trying to find a bra that gives me lift without ruining my whole f#$!ing day because it's so uncomfortable, you'd be within your rights to question my sanity.[5]

6. I once purchased a product called "Vitamin-C Facelift Patch."

7. I give myself pedicures once in a while so it was only a matter of time before Mari asked to have one too. So I washed her little feet, massaged them with aromatic cream and then painted her toenails. It was fun. Mari has also worn lipstick, sometimes borrowing mine, and sometimes improvising with illicitly gotten markers.

8. Have I pointed out to Mari how media manipulates us into believing in an unobtainable beauty ideal? When Mari was three, this would have been like explaining a space-time wormhole to her.

So what do you think? Should I rename this book *A Mother's Hypocrisy?*

I guess what I'm trying to say is that this is tricky. I'm not sure how to negotiate this contradiction and I never have been. It's well and fine to say looks aren't important, but where do I draw the line? Do I stop wearing makeup and moisturizing and establish a Meetup group to bring back bra-burning bonfires?[6] When

---

5 Buy an expensive uncomfortable bra once, shame on you. Buy an expensive uncomfortable bra seventy-five times, please shoot me.
6 Now say "bring back bra-burning bonfires" ten times fast.

does caring about your appearance end and being a slave to beauty begin? How do I teach my daughter to separate her feelings of self-worth from her appearance when I repeatedly fail to do so myself?

Opposite of Serious

When your daughter gets called beautiful, sometimes it's hard to know how to react. Here are a few pleasantries to keep in your pocket. The next time it happens, you'll be prepared. You're welcome!

How to Respond When Someone Calls Your Daughter "Beautiful"

Response #3

She's beautiful!

As beautiful as my resting bitch face?

Response #4

She's beautiful!

She doesn't get out of bed for less than $10,000 Haha I wish! She wakes up at 5 a.m.!

In 1990 Linda Evangelista said that supermodels like her don't get out of bed for less than $10,000.

If you remember that, you're probably as old as my mom.

Opposite of Serious

As I think I mentioned a few pages back, one day I got into the elevator of my building and saw my reflection without being prepared to do so. All I could see was my sagging jowls. This is nuts, I thought. Why do I see them and feel bad? Why can't I love my sagging jowls? That thought led to this humor piece, in which the narrator gets a little carried away.

A Woman's Attempt to Accept Herself Goes Awry

I first saw you in the mirror. I wasn't planning to see my reflection, so when I looked, unfiltered truth stared back at me. And there you were, the portent of Age. My drooping jowls. I hated you.

The second time I saw you, I was more prepared. I looked you square in the . . . I looked at you. I said, "I accept you. I welcome you. You and I have much in common. You are not my enemy."

The third time, I said, "I honor your wisdom. I admire your stories and accomplishments. I embrace the struggles you've witnessed and your courage in overcoming them. I will never try to hide you with an Alexander McQueen floral-print silk neckerchief."

The fourth time, slightly breathless, I said, "If falling for the force of gravity is wrong, I don't want to be right."

Then I told you that I loved you.

But you didn't say you loved me back.

It was mortifying. After everything we've been through, I felt we had a deep bond forged by shared experience and suffering. I assumed we'd reached an elevated state together where harsh, external judgments about beauty couldn't touch us—a world where airbrushing was for people who don't know Charlotte from Emily. I thought you loved me too. I was wrong. You're just as shallow as everyone else.

After that, I have to be honest—I started looking at other wrinkles. My crow's-feet are warm and compassionate and obviously open to a relationship. So what if I don't have the same feelings toward them? At least they don't just sit there like some unhinged collagen fiber, expecting me to do all the work.

My nasolabial folds are fun and full of enthusiasm. They're always suggesting something surprising, like waking up at four a.m. to watch the sunrise together from a hot air balloon or building a fort out of tongue depressors. They make me feel alive.

I don't have to tell you about my glabellar lines—I suspect you've always been a little jealous of them. Silent, muscular and passionate. Believe me, they're not just trying to hide lack of substance beneath taciturnity. They've blown my mind on more than one occasion. Sorry if that hurts you to hear it. And in case you were wondering, elasticity does matter.

Did I mention that a friend was telling me about the benefits of sea plankton the other day? No?

Oh, God, listen to me—I've become such a vindictive bitch. I don't want to live this way. I'd rather be emotionally vulnerable than bitter and closed to love. I refuse to let you have that power over me.

No response? What exactly are you trying to say?

Oh, I get it. You think you're making me stronger by hurting me. Thanks, but I can do that all by myself. What I need from you is support and nonjudgment. I would have thought that the one place I could find that was in the mirror. What a fool I was.

Well, I've got news for you. *(Soundtrack music.)* I won't stop living just because my sebaceous glands are underproducing essential oils that women believe you can purchase for $475 in a

1.35-ounce bottle. *(Soundtrack music with rainstorm.)* Maybe I'm crazy but what I've come to realize is that we're put on this earth for a purpose and that purpose doesn't just end because you have the time and the money to book a cruise when you're in the mood to go on one. And maybe you didn't notice this, but I'm a woman. This may come as a shock to you and to all the haters who dismiss me because Selena Gomez and Demi Lovato seem like the same person to me. We don't stop loving because our dermis begins to thin. Our dermis begins to thin because we stop loving.

My Life in Pink:
BEAUTY BULLET POINTS

The pending question: How do I teach my daughter to separate her feelings of self-worth from her appearance when I fail to do so myself?

Ahead of Mari's adolescence, I'm attempting to parse this issue—the whole "fucked-up female beauty and body image" thing. Let's start by outlining a few universal truths, apart from Jane Austen's one about a single man with expendable income wanting a wife.[7] Here they are:

- Women are judged by their looks far more than men.

It's why things like Spanx exist. It's why women journalists on TV used to get fired after they reached middle age, while their male counterparts became respected, well-paid elders. It's why Prince Charming liked Cinderella and why Prince Charming

---

7 And then wanting a second wife when the first one isn't young anymore.

liked Snow White and why that other prince liked Aurora. I could go on, but you get the picture.

• Women care about their looks far more than men.

It's why women spend hundreds of billions of dollars on beauty products every year. It's why Robert Redford, born in 1936, gets to look like he's in his seventies, while Jane Fonda, born 1937, doesn't. It's why last week I bought a pair of boots I didn't need because the fringe tassels hypnotized me into handing over my credit card. I could go on but you get the picture.

Here's a picture of the boots,
in case you didn't get the picture.

Which of these universal truths came first, however? Do women care about their looks because we're judged more for our appearance? Or are we just like that naturally? Why do women care about their looks? Ready for some more bullet points?

Women spend more time on their looks because:

- We want to attract men.

- We are in competition with each other.

- We want to feel good about ourselves.

Let's start with wanting to attract men. There's nothing wrong with that, particularly if you're heterosexual. Personally, I like men. In my early twenties, I wished I didn't because though I desired them sexually, I couldn't find one I respected and felt attracted to all at the same time. Also, when I actually wanted a man, I wasn't very good at attracting them. I was an awkward introvert with poor flirting skills. My ineptness notwithstanding, there's nothing wrong with wanting to attract a man. That's part of what makes babies.

However, while men *do* fall for stuff like high heels and red lips, many are also attracted to openness, confidence and power.[8] So if you're a lady looking for a man, ask yourself which qualities you'd like to cultivate—becoming more open and confident and empowered, or spending time and energy and focus and money on antiwrinkle luminizing revitalizing nourishing hydrating replenishing smoothing radiant vital color-correcting face serum foam lotion gel cream? It's totally your call and I'm not judging you either way, but a 1.7-ounce jar of serum foam lotion gel cream costs about $105 and doesn't work anyway.

Moving on to the second reason women spend more time on their looks—because we're in competition with each other. There

---

8 Matt once told me that when he was younger, he had sexual fantasies about Margaret Thatcher. "Okay," I said, "it was nice knowing you." But it turns out this was a *thing* and lots of British men his age fantasized about the former prime minister. Isn't that wonderfully loony and British?

is something wrong with that. The evolutionary biology theory is that we're wired to undercut each other because once upon a time we competed for sperm. But ladies, we can *evolve*, can't we? Even Barbie evolved[9] and she's made entirely of plastic. We women, flesh and blood and conscience, can do better. When women compete with each other, it's bad for us personally and collectively. We end up locked in the tower instead of going to the ball, for example. When we love and help each other, however, we can use our magical powers to reverse the eternal winter. We'll talk more about women competing with each other later.

Finally, the third reason women spend more time on their looks is that we want to feel good about ourselves. This one is also okay. In her book *The Beauty Myth*—which analyzes how images of beauty damage women—Naomi Wolf makes the distinction between a woman who chooses what she wants to look like and one who allows others, like men or the advertising industry, to choose for her.

> I am not attacking anything that makes women feel good; only what makes us feel bad in the first place. We all like to be desirable and feel beautiful.

That's a quote from *The Beauty Myth* and it's an important distinction. You can burn your bra or not. The point is that you should figure out what *you* want rather than let anyone else dictate your wants or override your own needs. Figuring out your own motivation for buying something or shaving something or smearing something on your face is a good thing to do and I will try to understand what's driving my own impulses so that Mari can learn to do the same.

---

9 When Barbie was finally introduced with different body shapes and skin tones in 2016, the Mattel campaign was called #TheDollEvolves.

I've also revised my list of what I'm going to teach my daughter. Here it is.

1. We live in a society in which some people will try to make you feel bad and inadequate. They are idiots.

2. Figure out what *you* want and take it from there.

That's it.

Here's something else Naomi Wolf said:

> For I conclude that the enemy is not lipstick, but guilt itself; that we deserve lipstick, if we want it, *and* free speech; we deserve to be sexual *and* serious—or whatever we please; we are entitled to wear cowboy boots to our own revolution.

Personally, I will be wearing these.

Princess Studies 101:
PHOTOSHOPPED FOR YOGA SOCKS

The way the beauty industry manipulates, exploits and exhausts women is the subject of *The Beauty Myth* by Naomi Wolf, published in 1991. That same year, *Backlash: The Undeclared War Against American Women* by Susan Faludi was also published, chronicling the backlash that eroded the achievements of the feminist movement. *Backlash* includes a chapter about the beauty industry in the 1980s, and how it promoted a "return to femininity" and encouraged the idea that "women's professional progress had downgraded their looks; equality had created worry lines and cellulite." Faludi illustrates how the campaigns that sprang from that idea have had a destructive impact on women.

Though both books were bestsellers and considered seminal, little has changed. Scratch that. The way the beauty industry affects women has gotten worse.

If you feel like killing some time, search YouTube for "Photoshopped model before and after." It's astonishing. Women whose job it is to be beautiful and skinny in the first place are made even skinnier, their features manipulated to look ever more cartoonlike—eyes enlarged, skin tone smoothed, cheekbones raised, hair thickened, bottoms made perky and boobs made spectacular.

Some more food for thought: The cosmetics industry earns more than $50 billion annually in the United States. Cosmetic surgery has exploded as an industry since *The Beauty Myth* and *Backlash* were written, with hundreds of thousands of boob jobs, liposuctions and tummy tucks each year dotting the landscape of body shapes. Eighty percent of all ten-year-old girls have been on a diet, according to a 2010 study.[10] Fifty-three percent of thirteen-year-old girls are unhappy with their bodies, and by the age of seventeen the number increases to 78 percent, according to the same study.

Study after study supports the same thesis: When women are constantly exposed to unrealistic images of idealized feminine beauty—airbrushed, Photoshopped images of women transformed to look like Barbie dolls and porn stars—it erodes our self-esteem. Most women say they would change something about their body or face. Most women believe they carry too much weight. In general, women don't feel "good enough" when it comes to the way we look, and we consequently spend valuable time and energy and resources to improve our appearance without ever feeling we've fixed the problem of our imperfect faces, bodies and hair.

And what about Little Princesses?

The relevant studies have examined the reactions of adolescent girls, teenagers and adult women to beauty images. In 2009, researchers at the University of Central Florida did something a little different—they conducted a study on very young girls.[11] Girls aged three to six were shown videos of beautiful, thin princesses in animated movies and were evaluated afterward. The study mirrored those done on older girls and women in which self-esteem was affected by images of airbrushed, too-skinny, too-beautiful women. But in the case of the three- to six-year-

---

10 K. Hepworth, "Eating disorders today—not just a girl thing," *Journal of Christian Nursing* 27, no. 3 (2010).
11 S. Hayes and S. Tantleff-Dunn, "Am I too fat to be a princess? Examining the effects of popular children's media on young girls' body image," *British Journal of Developmental Psychology* 28, pt. 2 (2009).

olds, exposure to these videos did not affect their behavior or self-esteem.

Interesting, right?

If you're the parent of a Little Princess, perhaps you're not surprised by the results of this study. You might have noticed something about your daughter that I've observed in mine. When Mari watches the princesses, she *becomes* a princess. When she puts on a princess dress, she feels like she *is* a princess. She's not less beautiful or special. She feels fabulous when she watches princesses and when she dresses as them. Her imagination isn't constricted by reality and her confidence has not been battered by Disney or fashion magazine waistlines.

When we see the Photoshopped models, we see everything we aren't. When Little Princesses see images of beautiful women, they see themselves.

Of course, this is just a reprieve, because the pattern changes and reverses in adolescence. If only we teenagers and adult women could harness that toddler confidence. If only we could look at the Photoshopped images and not internalize the message that we aren't good enough. Let's all agree to work on that, because if we can project the kind of self-love that Little Princesses possess, it would certainly have a positive influence on our daughters as they grow up.

Another strategy against the detrimental effects of the beauty industry is to let our kids in on the secret. When Cai was six years old, we showed him an advertisement featuring a beautiful woman that was promoting either a car or a watch or a crappy beer—I forget which.

"Isn't it silly?" we told him. "What does this woman have to do with what they're selling? And people fall for it and actually drive this/wear this/drink this crappy beer just because there's a pretty woman in the picture!"

Cai totally got it. He saw that it was funny and understood how advertisers try to manipulate us. Soon he started finding advertising absurdities and pointing them out to us, like how milk is sold using images of busty beautiful women, or how men's cologne is sold using images of mostly naked beautiful women, or how yoga socks are sold using images of completely naked beautiful women. Except for their yoga socks.

Mari is not yet six and we haven't introduced her to the concept of media and advertising manipulations, but we will. And even though Cai got the joke, I know it's more complicated for girls, at whom these images are chiefly directed.

I can't change the beauty industry or the advertising industry or the ongoing backlash again feminism. All I can do is let Mari in on the joke when she's older, and eventually explain why the joke is so often not funny. I can show her the absurd Photoshopping and the disturbing statistics on eating disorders and tell her how all the pressures on girls and women are designed to deplete and hold girls back from reaching their potential. I can encourage her to stay constantly aware as she's bombarded with image after image of unattainable beauty.

Mari's a smart girl. I hope she'll get the hustle and then she can make her own decisions about what to do with it. But like with everything else, I can't control what will happen. Our Little Princesses will one day realize that they are not really princesses, and they'll be vulnerable to all this lunacy. Much as I don't want to, I have to let this one go too.

Opposite of Serious

How would we ever survive without "dos and don'ts" articles? Aren't they the best?

Pedicure Dos and Don'ts

A good pedicure can brighten your day and make you feel pampered, energized and ready to expose your feet to the general public and the guy who just swiped right and resembles Zac Efron. Get the most out of your pedicure experience by following these essential tips.

■ <u>Don't</u> let the technician begin without first taking a good look around and assessing the cleanliness of the salon. Are there steam sterilizers for the utensils? Do they use pumice stones, which can never truly be disinfected without ethanol, oxygen-rich blue flames and a dip in the *mikveh*? Does it look like a place in which fungus would feel happy?

■ <u>Don't</u> soak your feet in the footbath. You were probably hoping to relax during this forty-five minutes of your day, but, sadly, bacteria and viruses and other infectious microbes fester in most salon footbaths. These organisms will colonize your skin and cause boils and rashes and even the odd fatal staph infection.

■ <u>Don't</u> shower, bathe or do sports within twenty-four hours of having your pedicure or the nails will chip and lose their luster. Instead take that time to read a women's magazine and consider the beauty industry's recommendations for how to spend your hard-earned cash. Like the $30 you just dropped on the pedicure.

■ Don't pretend that applying the periwinkle polish to your toenails isn't a symptom of your need to control everything. It is, but unlike everything else in this dark-night-of-the-soul universe, selecting the exact shade that will complement your new halter dress does actually fall into your sphere of dominion. Great choice, by the way! Vanessa Hudgens totally wore the same color with Zac Efron on her arm at the *Vanity Fair* Oscar party.

■ Don't ask too many questions about the working conditions of the women who staff the salon. While you're doing that, absolutely never Google that article about the twelve-hour shifts, the below-minimum wages and what happened to an immigrant worker when a splash of nail polish remover landed on one of her customers' Prada sandals.

■ Don't spend too much time appraising the toenails of the men in your life, whose maintenance costs zero dollars and zero cents and are likely au naturel and fancy-free.

■ Don't start wondering about the patriarchy and the advertising industry that has manipulated you into investing valuable time and resources and energy into the shell that is your body rather than the fire that is your soul.

■ Don't imagine that when you peel back the layers of your need to have your feet looking perfect, you won't discover a primitive female *Homo sapiens* who's competing for premium sperm without ever stopping to ask why or who benefits or how pedicures went from an occasional indulgence to a weekly obligation.

■ Don't agonize over the fact that some women have been indoctrinated to believe feminism is actually a bad thing, while others have willingly forsaken feminism in favor of $180 bird poop facials and waxing their pubes.

■ Don't launch a Change.org campaign for women to redirect all future pedicure expenses, but also money that was previously earmarked for primers, concealers, foundations, bronzers, balms, glosses, powders, toners, exfoliators, gels, sprays, pomades, foams, shapers, sculptors, butters, mousses, stain-blasting strips, mists, fiber pastes, styling puddings, for realz I am not making any of this up, beauty water, creams, crèmes, serums, scrubs, muds, pore perfectors, capsules, masks, blotting tissues, glow enhancers, microderm-abrasions, anti-aging restorative revitalizing correcting radiance cellular power luminating ultra lift brightening firming hydro-plumping f%#!ing everything, toward a scholarship fund for the women working as underpaid pedicurists and anyone else working for too little wages in the beauty industry.

■ Don't be surprised when your campaign is featured in *People* magazine and catches the interest of Emma Watson, who becomes an advocate for the movement and whose retweet of your "Calluses are sexier than ignorance" missive leads to the account reaching 214K followers.

■ Don't say no to the book deal, the speaking tour and the high-profile publicity event, which will attract celebs like George and

Amal but also Zac Efron, who I heard is single again. Don't forget to buy a new dress and shoes and have some Botox and Adderall and shave *all the things* for the occasion. As you'll be wearing sandals, you know what else not to forget to do. Go on—you totally deserve this!

■ When getting your pedicure, *do* leave a generous tip! Salon workers genuinely appreciate this, since some even get to keep a percentage of their gratuities. Twenty percent is recommended—more if you've gotten a really awesome pedicure.

✦ ✦ ✦

Interesting Little Princess Fact #4

Like many Little Princesses, before she outgrew them Mari insisted on nighttime Pull-Ups with the image of a princess. Winnie the Pooh, Buzz Lightyear and Minnie Mouse were all unacceptable images for Mari to pee on. She would only pee on a princess. It was the principle of the thing.

✦ ✦ ✦

Little Princess Pie

Jamie Apuzzo gets to wear a sparkly headband each time she agrees to sit quietly for five minutes. She earns a new rhinestone barrette whenever she descends a flight of stairs without trying to fly. Her princess toddler canopy bed was purchased after the completion of her first and only "calm and gentle" sticker chart.

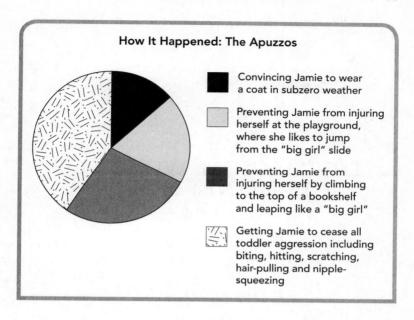

How It Happened: The Apuzzos

Convincing Jamie to wear a coat in subzero weather

Preventing Jamie from injuring herself at the playground, where she likes to jump from the "big girl" slide

Preventing Jamie from injuring herself by climbing to the top of a bookshelf and leaping like a "big girl"

Getting Jamie to cease all toddler aggression including biting, hitting, scratching, hair-pulling and nipple-squeezing

"The really vexing thing is that a minute after we put them on, Jamie takes off the headbands and the barrettes and then refuses to put them back on," her mother said, "so her hair is always in her face. She also makes a tent with two chairs and a sheet and then sleeps under it every night, so she never even uses the canopy bed."

Chapter 5

THE MAGICAL WORLD OF
THE DISNEY DOLLAR

My Life in Pink:
SOFIA THE FIRST, DISNEY COLLECTOR
AND *THE BRADY BUNCH*

I watched so much crappy television as a kid that if I were to tell my kids, "Don't watch that crap," I'd immediately be awarded the Stupid Parent of the Year medal by the president.[1]

(Canned laughter.)

Sure, I'd like them not to watch at all, but if they *are* watching, I want them to see useful, educational shows, in which Cookie Monster teaches them how to count and Jack Bauer teaches them how to kill with a clean punch to the heart.

I don't want them watching dumb shows like I did, because I know firsthand what a titanic waste of time it is. I'm pretty sure

---

1 The president of Crazyland.

I spent the 1970s in an anodyne fog of sitcoms and antihista-
mines. History repeats itself, however, and when Mari was a toddler her second-favorite show was *Sofia the First*.

For the uninitiated:

> *Sofia the First is a girl from the village who was doing all right*
> *Then she became a princess overnight*
> *She's finding out*
> *what being royal's all about.*
> *I could go on paraphrasing this theme song,*
> *but Disney will sue me, it won't be long!*

You get the gist. Sofia is a regular little girl who becomes a
princess and is periodically visited by all the Disney princesses—
Cinderella shows up in the pilot episode, and Jasmine, Aurora
and the rest eventually make cameos to help Sofia through some
pickle. If that isn't enough to make you hate this show, there are
also musical numbers.[2]

In other words, Sofia the First is Little Princess Valium.

Did the Disney money spinners get together with the sole
purpose of creating a show to target princess-obsessed girls?
It wasn't enough that our daughters were crazy for Cinderella
and Aurora and Jasmine. There had to be an even more relatable
character for Little Princesses to worship. Because once they
created Sofia, Disney was well positioned to sell the following:

---

2 My college roommate was a wonderful person whose only flaw was
  that she played the *Sunday in the Park with George* soundtrack every
  day. Musicals have held a special place of resentment in my heart ever
  since.

Sofia the First Musical Jewelry Box

Sofia the First Talking Magical Amulet

Sofia the First Tiara[3]

Sofia the First Magical Talking Castle

Sofia the First Talking Enchanted Vanity

Sofia the First Play-Doh Amulet and Jewels and Vanity Set

Sofia the First MP3 Sing-Along Boom Box
with Microphone[4]

Sofia the First Princess-in-Training Headphones
with Built-in Tiara

And that's just a partial list of toys. There are also Sofia the First twin sheet sets, water bottles, backpacks, rugs, window curtains and shower curtains, and there's a purple playtime chair, an upholstered chair, a table and chair set, a toddler bed, a tent, and a tricked-out, battery-powered convertible car. And so much other stuff that won't fit on this page.

Disney should have skipped the show. Why put all that effort into plot and production? They should just make videos showcasing all the stuff they want us to buy for our Little Princesses.

Oh, wait a minute. Someone already did that.

More than one person. Thousands of people are doing it, in fact. And millions of people are watching them. I'm talking, of course, about unboxers, the people who take videos of their hands opening new stuff and then post them on YouTube. It's a huge industry and an exploding genre.

---

3 Least surprising item on the list.
4 Boom box is shaped like a handbag.

Yes, this is actually considered a *genre*. And *that* was Mari's favorite show as a toddler. Mari loved unboxing even more than *Sofia the First*. Specifically, she loved Disney Collector, that Play-Doh–mushing, Kinder Egg–unwrapping, MagiClip doll–worshipping enigma wrapped in an immaculate Hello Kitty manicure.

It's pretty kooky and I don't get it. A gazillion little kids disagree, however, and so do adults—unboxing is also popular among plenty of people over the age of three. The number of iPhone 6 unboxings was so huge that there's a whole meme of videos mocking them. As of this writing I don't have a smartphone, which gives you some indication of why I'm stymied. I'm hanging on to the past for dear life, checking Facebook excessively only when I'm at my monitor. Please excuse me for a few minutes . . .

I'm back. If I was an infectious disease, I'd be chlamydia. Oh, Internet, what did I ever do without you?

Where was I? That's right—Disney Collector. I think I may have already mentioned her in this book, mostly because Mari's obsession with her dovetailed with the whole princess thing.

Hey, guys.[5] I was wrong about *Sofia the First*. *This* is Little Princess Valium: a woman's hands playing with Play-Doh and dolls and other toys, her voice slightly nasal yet charming, her Brazilian accent saying things like, "Too bad we're gonna have to hide these adorable boots."[6]

For about a year, whenever Mari got her hands on Play-Doh,

---

5 "Hey, guys" is Disney Collector's signature phrase.
6 That's a line from the classic Disney Collector video "Play Doh Sparkle Princess Ariel Elsa Anna Disney Frozen MagiClip Glitter Glider Magic Clip Dolls," which has been viewed a mere 545 million times.

she slapped a brown wad[7] onto her Princess Anna MagiClip doll's feet and said, "Too bad I have to hide these adorable boots."

Mari was mesmerized by Disney Collector. When she watched a "DC" video, her little hands wiggled as if she were playing with the toys too. Maybe this was more like Little Princess virtual reality. Or perhaps the combination of repetition paired with princesses and Play-Doh was simply too compelling for a three-year-old to resist. I'd analyze it, but in the end I just needed to treat it like any addictive activity. I let Mari have it in doses, and after she'd had her fix I had to be ruthless. There are several phrases I never imagined myself saying when I was twenty-two and listening to Nirvana. "Absolutely no more Disney Collector today!" is one of them.

Sadly, though I regret all the *Brady Bunch* I consumed, I wasn't disciplined enough to say, "No Disney Collector ever again." I let Mari watch. And then wrote a series of top 10 lists to shake the glitter out. Here they are.

Opposite of Serious

Top 10 Rejected *Sofia the First* Plotlines

1. During a special Princess School flying derby match, Princess Sofia falls off her pony, Minimus. She agrees to apply a plain beige Band-Aid to the boo-boo.

---

7 All our Play-Doh is brown because Mari mashes the colors together, which is so sad for a Little Princess.

2. All of Princess Sofia's underwear is in the laundry. Princess Amber worries they will be late for the village fair. When Prince James offers to lend Sofia a pair of his underpants, Sofia discovers they are blue! But, remembering how much Amber wants to go to the fair, and mindful of the concept of time, Sofia says yes.

3. A witch has placed a hex on Sofia's sippy cup and it has started to leak. After a musical number, Sofia volunteers to drink water from an old gray sports bottle used by Fauna during her aerobicise years.

4. When all of Cedric's magical powers fail to remove the bits of sparkly confetti from the palace floor, Sofia concedes that glitter must forevermore be banned from the Kingdom of Enchancia.

5. Sofia is confused about what it means to be a real princess. Belle, Cinderella, Jasmine, Ariel and Aurora make special guest appearances to help her through her *Lebenskrise*. When Sofia asks why Snow White has not come with them, the other princesses all roll their eyes and whisper to one another, "What do you think? Should we tell her about the botched Botox?"

6. On Sofia's birthday, Cedric concocts a special pink elixir that causes everyone to feel fuzzy and laugh raucously whenever King Roland makes one of his "jokes." However, the beverage causes Clover to behave in an irrational and erratic manner. Sofia wonders how such a sweet, cute, beautiful, adorable and gorgeous little being whom she loves to pieces can suddenly turn into the devil.[8] Meanwhile, Flora, Fauna and Merryweather make plans to produce the pink drink in large quantities in the trolls' grotto.

---

8 That is a metaphor for the toddler years.

7. Amber has fallen into a trance! Sofia discovers her, zombielike, watching the image of hands with whimsically painted fingernails opening jars of sparkling Play-Doh and fashioning them into after-party cocktail dresses. Sofia must break the spell before the Enchanted Feast of the Tri-Kingdom dinner. Amber finally snaps out of it when she is offered a cookie.

8. It's Wassailia, a vague yet recognizable winter holiday that hopefully won't offend anyone. Will Sofia find the perfect gift for Baileywick or will she spend countless hours jostling with other Enchancia shoppers, sweaty and depleted, battling for the last Glitter Glider MagiClip doll? Some princess you've sort of heard of makes a special appearance in this memorable holiday special.

9. Inspired by her amulet, Sofia makes yogurt pops, which color everything, including her skin, electric purple. The Flying Pageant will start soon and Sofia is running out of time. Baileywick, the steward, tells her to "make it work."

10. Sofia's vanity set—which includes a comb, brush, hand mirror and lip gloss—is lost. Clover tries to find it, but slips on the AquaDoodle drawing mat before sliding across the magnetic memo board, only to trip on the talking tea party set as the reflection refracted by the snow globe tumbler with the matching spiral straw blinds him. Finally, he lands on a sharp tiara and Sofia understands that Cedric has put a hex on her. In order to break the curse, Sofia must give up her exorbitantly priced nighttime Pull-Ups so that her mother, Miranda, can start saving to buy the pair of bronze Enzo Angiolini peep-toe pumps that will give her life meaning.

Top 10 Ways to Make Disney Collector Your Friend

Hey, guys! If your daughter is like mine, she loves unboxing even more than Sofia the First. *The whole Disney Collector phenomenon raises important questions, like "What did she do with all that chocolate?" and also "How can I bear watching even one more Disney Collector video?"*

Don't despair. Disney Collector isn't your nemesis. The next time your daughter says, "I want to watch Disney Collector," try some of these ideas, which are designed to teach important lessons to your little one and improve your life. As Humphrey Bogart said before he mushed black Play-Doh into the shape of a falcon, "This could be the beginning of a beautiful friendship."

1. The "Play-Doh Lunchtime Creations" video.
Use this video as a way to get your toddler to eat. Be sure to explain that when you say the word "eat," you're not referring to actual Play-Doh. Or dirt. Or sand.

2. The "Peppa Pig Blocks Mega Hospital Building Playset with Ambulance" video.
See if you can use this one to impress upon your toddler the importance of never sticking her wet finger into the electrical socket, lest she end up injured in an overcrowded ward like George Pig.

3. The "Disney Princess Ariel Water Palace Bath Playset" video.
Use this video as a way to demonstrate how objects—such as the homemade flotation device Disney Collector makes for Elsa and Anna—float when they are less dense than the fluid in which they are sitting. Then say, "It's science!"

4. Use Disney Collector's voice as a model for your next audition.
Because it's your dream to play the role of a tender-hearted Brazilian woman who stands by her bossa nova–singing boyfriend.

5. Use Disney Collector as a reminder to moisturize your hands.
Because hers are fabulous, especially when she uses that dizzying fast-forward function and her fingers look like they're on speed.

6. And get your nails done while you're at it.
Even though you will never get your Hello Kitty manicure as perfect as Disney Collector's.

7. The "Play Doh McDonald's Restaurant Playset with Cookie Monster" video.
Use this one as evidence that fast food—including the star-shaped chicken nuggets your kid demands every day—should only be eaten sparingly. You might want to point out how unappetizing that brown Play-Doh burger looks, even to a toddler who likes to eat playground sand.

8. The "Play Doh Mega Fun Factory Playset" video.
This one is a good illustration of why factory workers must unionize. *Wait. What?*

9. The "Cookie Monster Pool Party with Mermaid Elsa Mermaid Anna" video.
Use this one the next time you trip on acid.

10. Any one of the Surprise Egg videos that have been viewed more than 10 million times.

Finally, use these as an opportunity to ask yourself WTF is happening to the human race. Because people are choosing to spend their valuable time watching unboxing videos.

Top 10 Tangential Things About *Sofia*

1. *Sofia*'s creators imagined a Tim Gunn soundalike for the role of Baileywick before hiring Tim Gunn.

2. The actress behind Sofia's voice is Ariel Winter, who also plays the brainy daughter Alex on *Modern Family*.

3. Ariel Winter's costar on *Modern Family* is also called Sofia, or rather Sofía, but Sofía Vergara and Sofia the First have never met in real life.

4. Sofía Vergara is Latina. Sofia the First is not Latina, even though a *Sofia* producer originally said she was. It caused a minor kerfuffle.

5. The Amulet of Avalor was designed by Harry Winston, and Richard Burton originally bought it for Elizabeth Taylor, which is the real reason why Cedric is so obsessed with it.

6. Sofia is the capital of Bulgaria.

7. One rumor has it that Sofia's biological father is Barry Manilow. Another suggests that her father is actually Nicolas Cage.

8. Sofia the First and Jake the Pirate used to date when they were in the Mickey Mouse Club together. They are no longer on speaking terms even though they're forced to perform together in the Disney Junior Live Pirate and Princess Adventure.

9. My son, Cai, asked for the Fisher-Price Jake and the Never Land Pirates ship minutes before he lost interest in the show. Mari plays with it, though, and sometimes puts her princesses on it.

10. Dora the Explorer once reportedly called Sofia "that stupid, vacant eggplant." A representative for Dora did not respond to a request to comment on the incident.

Princess Studies 101: DISNEY PRINCESS DOLLAR TIMELINE

So how much cash do the princesses generate for Disney? Enough to buy and sell Arendelle a thousand times. If the Duke of Weselton wanted to get rich, he should have just bought Disney stock. It's impossible to calculate every dollar the princesses have earned, but here's a timeline with some of the highlights.

1937

Snow White and the Seven Dwarfs is the first full-length animated feature released in movie theaters.

People thought Walt Disney was nuts to release a full-length animated film. Until then he'd produced shorts, and *Snow White* cost him $1.5 million, which was four times as much money as he'd budgeted. But the movie became a huge box office success, earning $6.5 million by 1939. Snow White is the third most profitable Disney princess, according to *Time* magazine, and her movie comes in at #1 in overall box office sales according to the *Fiscal Times*.[9]

1950

Cinderella is released after a series of box office flops—during which Disney was on the verge of bankruptcy.

This was Disney's biggest hit since *Snow White* and is credited with saving Walt Disney Studios. Cinderella is the second most profitable princess and ranks #2 among princesses at the box office.

---

9 Rankings of princess profitability appeared in *Time* magazine and were originally calculated by Terapeak.com, which based the rankings on eBay sales since 2013. The box office/ticket sales rankings appeared in the *Fiscal Times* in 2014 and include rerelease profits, which is why *Frozen*—released just a year earlier—didn't top the list at the time.

1959

Sleeping Beauty is released and initially considered a failure.

 The film's lackluster box office performance might be one reason Disney took a lengthy princess hiatus. Subsequent film releases and merchandising redeemed Aurora's worth, however, and she's ranked #7 on the profitable princess list and #6 on the princess box office sales list.

1970s

Still no princess movies.

 But my family and I went to Walt Disney World in Orlando a few times during this decade, and theatrical rereleases of the Sleepy Trio earned Disney lots of Princess Dollars.

1982

Still no princess movies, but Disney dusts off Cinderella's attic cobwebs and uses a clip of her transformation in *A Disney Christmas Gift*, a TV special that airs on CBS.

 At the time, I was in the sixth grade and my classmates and I were each assigned a country about which we had to write a school report. I got Denmark. This was exciting for me because I associated the country with *The Ugly Duckling*, one of my favorite childhood books. Its author was Danish and, incidentally, the same person who penned *The Little Mermaid*.

 See what I did there? The Danish writer to whom I'm referring is of course Hans Christian Andersen, who also wrote *The Snow Queen*, which became the basis for another Disney film.[10]

---

10 It's *Frozen*. I'm talking about *Frozen*.

You know who else loved Hans Christian Andersen? Walt Disney. It's almost like he could see into the future, because Andersen wrote the story that would be adapted into Disney's biggest film ever.

 You know what else happened in 1982? Epcot Center opened at Walt Disney World in Orlando. Is that important? Not really. But it does foreshadow the last entry of this timeline.

1986–1994

Disney releases the Sleepy Trio films on home video.

 At first Disney lagged in the home video market for fear it would cheapen the brand, but the company finally released *Sleeping Beauty* in 1986, *Cinderella* in 1988 and *Snow White* in 1994. The videos were all megahits and have earned Disney hundreds of millions of Princess Dollars.

1989

Maelstrom opens.

 Maelstrom isn't a princess film and, again, this is just a bit of foreshadowing for your reading pleasure. Maelstrom was a ride that opened at the Norwegian Pavilion at Disney

World's Epcot Center, which took visitors on a boat to seek "the spirit of Norway." Sadly for Norway enthusiasts, however, Maelstrom was doomed. So if you're time traveling definitely check out this ride while there's still time!

1989

The Little Mermaid, Disney's first princess film in three decades, is released.

After Walt Disney died in 1966, the company struggled throughout the '70s and '80s, but Princess Ariel was hugely popular and the movie was part of a new string of animated hits for Disney. *Time* ranks Ariel the fifth most profitable princess and the *Fiscal Times* puts *The Little Mermaid* at #10 for princess ticket sales.

A princess saves Disney again! The irony isn't subtle anymore—it's yelling shrilly. "Shrill" is a label traditionally used to silence women.

1991

Beauty and the Beast is released.

 This movie, with its Broadway-style music, was a huge moneymaker for Disney. Belle comes in at #11 on *Time's* profitable princess list and #5 on the *Fiscal Times* box office sales list.

The book *The Beauty Myth* was also published that year. Just sayin'.

1992

Aladdin is released.

 The *Los Angeles Times* reported that when this film—which featured Princess Jasmine—passed the $200 million mark at the box office, it became the first animated film to ever do so and joined a then exclusive list of thirteen films to accomplish this moneymaking feat. Jasmine comes in at #9 on the princess profitability list and #4 in box office sales.

1995

Pocahontas is released.

The *Daily News* reported that prerelease Pocahontas merchandising included 6,500 Burger King restaurants "bedecked with posters promoting the movie and the 50 million Pocahontas figurines to be included in kids' meals" as well as Pocahontas dolls, bow and arrow sets, clothes, party packs, games, stuffed figures, shoes, books, chocolate bars, Hallmark cards, car giveaways, a Cheerios tie-in, and the soundtrack, which included the Academy Award–winning "Colors of the Wind." It also had the biggest premiere in movie history, at New York City's Central Park, with 100,000 people attending.

At around this time, Disney started to earn $1 billion in licensed merchandising from hits like *Aladdin*, *Beauty and the Beast*, *The Lion King* and *Pocahontas*.

Pocahontas does not appear in *Time*'s profitable princess list, but the movie is #8 on the *Fiscal Times* princess box office list. In general, the nonwhite princesses do not sell as much merchandise as the white ones.

1998

Mulan is released.

 Shortly after its release, the *Los Angeles Daily News* reported, "Disney's latest animated movie *Mulan* has revived the fortunes of its most precious division following several years of less-than-stellar performances. With $84.8 million in domestic grosses in its first three weeks through Thursday, *Mulan* has outperformed expectations and should be hugely profitable for the entertainment giant."

 Despite its success, *Mulan* did not make the *Time* list or the *Fiscal Times* list.

2000

A Disney executive goes to a Disney on Ice show and notices that the little girls in the audience are wearing homemade dresses.[11]

---

11 Originally reported in *Cinderella Ate My Daughter* by Peggy Orenstein.

The Disney exec, named Andy Mooney, realized that Disney was missing a merchandising opportunity and Disney soon began marketing the princesses together as a brand. This was the birth of the "princess culture" as we know it, and that's kind of where the story of this Little Princess book begins. But where does it end?

1999–2008

No "original" princess movies are made, but *Pocahontas II*, *The Little Mermaid II*, *Cinderella II*, *Mulan II*, *Cinderella III* and *The Little Mermaid III* are released.

2009

The Princess and the Frog is released.

 This is the last traditionally animated Disney princess film unless whoever succeeds current Disney chairman Bob Iger is a nostalgia fiend.

The film, featuring the first black Disney princess, was profitable, but like other nonwhite princesses, Tiana is less popular than the white ones. She ranks as #10 on the *Time* most popular list.

 We took Cai to Disneyland Paris in 2010 (see "Auberge de Cendrillon" on page 125) and happened to see the "New Generations" show featuring Tiana, even though I had no idea there was a new princess film because I didn't have a Little Princess yet. Perhaps absorbing the princess aura, however, Mari was conceived one month after that trip.

2010

Tangled is released.

 Rapunzel was Disney's first computer-animated princess. The movie earned $576 million at the box office and is one of the highest-grossing animated films of all time (#25 on the all-time list). Rapunzel ranks #6 on the *Time* list and the movie is #9 on the *Fiscal Times* box office list.

2012

Sofia the First premieres on the Disney Junior channel with a one-hour special.

The show was indeed specifically written for preschoolers in mind and became an instant hit, along with *Doc McStuffins* and *Jake and the Never Land Pirates*.

Still 2012

Brave is released.

 Brave is a Pixar film, but Pixar is owned by Disney and the film made $539 million at the box office. Merida ranks #8 on the *Time* list and the movie is #7 on the *Fiscal Times* list.

 Merida is a strong heroine whose character was intended to inspire and empower girls, but after the film Disney gave her a makeover on its website. The new Merida was slimmer, and her eyes were wider, her cheekbones raised and her neckline lowered to reveal cleavage. Brenda Chapman, who cowrote and codirected *Brave*, lambasted Disney and was part of a successful Change.org campaign to restore Merida to her pre-cream-puff image. She sometimes appears with the other princesses in Disney marketing shots, though more often she's left out.

We are not done with 2012

Princess profits.

 The Disney princess franchise earned $3 billion in global sales and was crowned the #1 brand for bestselling entertainment products by the Licensing Letter, a trade publication. *Star Wars* came in at #2.

The year 2012 was a breakout year for Disney princesses. Surely it can't get any better than that, right? Hahahahahahahahahahahahaha!!! You all know what's about to happen.

2013

Frozen is released.

1939

Wait, what?

 This is a Disney timeline so let's allow for a little fantastical time travel.

After *Snow White*'s phenomenal success in 1937, Walt Disney planned to bring more fairy tales to the silver screen and was especially attracted to the stories of Hans Christian Andersen. In 1939, Walt gave *The Snow Queen*—based on an Andersen fairy tale—a production number, but the project never went forward. No one is sure why. Walt also started developing an animated version of Andersen's *The Little Mermaid.* That project was delayed and then shelved and then finally revived in the mid-1980s. Walt did make a version of Andersen's *The Ugly Duckling*, however, in 1931. Remember *The Ugly Duckling*? It was one of my favorite childhood stories. And Disney did finally make an animated version of *The Snow Queen* in 2013. We're almost there. Hang on to your sleds.

In the 1970s, legendary Disney animator Marc Davis designed an Enchanted Snow Palace ride for Disneyland, featuring a "Snow Princess." Plans for the ride also got shelved.

2013

Frozen is released.

Where do I begin? *Frozen* is the highest-grossing animated film of all time. As of this writing it is the fifth-highest-grossing film in box office history, with $1.3 billion in worldwide ticket sales, and it has earned almost the same amount in merchandising sales. Elsa ranks #1 on *Time*'s list and *Frozen* is #3 on the *Fiscal Times*, but that's only because that list was compiled in 2014. Thanks to *Frozen* merchandising sales, Disney's profits have soared beyond all expectations.

Why?

If you're reading this book, you know exactly why. You have seen this film and then seen it again and again and again. You probably own an Elsa singing doll or an Olaf pillow or a *Frozen*-themed lunch box, or all of those things together are currently occupying space in a *Frozen* dress-up trunk. You might have really splashed out and purchased a *Frozen* canopy bed or a patio set or a Power Wheels Jeep Wrangler. At the very least, you have a few *Frozen* sippy cups or a backpack or a T-shirt or two or twenty. You may have thrown a *Frozen* birthday party recently, with a "Pin the Carrot on Olaf" game and *Frozen* snowflake decorations and an Elsa cake and turquoise magic wands for party favors; and maybe your daughter dresses up as Elsa for Halloween and Carnivale and Purim and Eid al-Adha and other festive occasions like visits to the dentist and Costco and going to sleep. You are swimming in *Frozen*, you wake up to *Frozen* and you spend your days in a glacial cosmos of Anna and Elsa. You know the movie and the songs by heart and your daughter has learned the ABCs from Elsa and the faux white braid that is supposed to attach to your daughter's hair has become your dog's favorite chew toy. Your life is an Arendelle megalopolis, a deep, boundless crevasse of *Frozen*, an altar to Anna and Elsa, a shrine to a Disney film and to a staggering amount of its licensed merchandise.

And where has it all led? To dollars in Mickey Mouse's pockets, of course.

Yet even though I came into motherhood as a pink- and princess-hating feminist, I don't begrudge Disney. Why? That's kind of what this book is about.

2016

The Snow Queen finally gets her ride.

 A Frozen Ever After ride opened in Epcot Center, replacing the Maelstrom ride at the Norwegian Pavilion. (Did you manage to ride it during your recent time travel trip?) According to WPLG News in Florida, the wait time for the new *Frozen* ride reached five hours on the first day.

My Life in Pink:
AUBERGE DE CENDRILLON

When Cai was three years old, Matt's brother invited us to meet them at Disneyland Paris. His family lives in London and we were living in Jerusalem, so Paris seemed like a dreamy way to see them. Well, Paris-ish. Disneyland is outside the city, and it's extremely and profoundly different from Paris itself, but never mind.

Some of you might be shaking your heads because you know something I didn't at the time. Disney is wasted on three-year-olds. They can't walk the distances and are freaked out by the enormous Winnie the Poohs and Goofys randomly roaming the park. Cai liked It's a Small World well enough, but his favorite thing in the whole place was a wooden camel outside Aladdin's Enchanted Passage, which he climbed on and pretended to ride for about an hour. It was October, very cold, and Matt and I were astonished by the prices and the food quality. So close to Paris and yet so very, very far. We had to go to an American chain—Starbucks—just to get food that wasn't a hot dog, which just shows you how much Disney has effectively created Bizarro World within its Marne-la-Vallée borders.

Yet we had an okay time, because it was good to see my brother-in-law and family and because Wine. In the year leading up to this trip, I'd had two early miscarriages trying to conceive our second child, but by the time we got to Disney I was recovered and feeling positive about life again.

My niece was eight years old and into princesses, so my brother-in-law had reserved a table at the Princess Lunch. We followed suit, again overlooking good sense and exorbitant prices in favor of family hangout time.

The Disney Princess Lunch is held in the Auberge de Cendrillon in Fantasyland. Outside the Auberge, little girls took princess dresses out of garment bags and donned them ahead of entering. *That's funny,* I thought. *Who buys princess dresses for little girls?*

We lined up—for what good is Disney without lines?—and were finally admitted into the restaurant. Suzy and Perla (the mice from Cinderella) greeted the kids and took photos with them. I don't recall which princesses showed up at that meal, but the food was better than anything we'd consumed at Disney—it's an actual French meal, though Cai didn't eat a thing except raisins I had stashed in my bag and the dessert. I remember how gaga the little girls in the room were over the actresses dressed as princesses. I was snarky and judgmental the whole time, because I didn't have a daughter who'd drunk the pink Kool-Aid—just a gender-neutral toddler picking up raisins he'd dropped on the carpet and popping them in his mouth. At least we hoped they were raisins.

Flash forward. I'm sure you know where this is going. As you might recall from the timeline, Mari was born less than a year after that trip. After swearing I would never return, we returned to Disneyland Paris when Cai was eight and Mari four. There was no brother-in-law to lay the blame on this time, just some new circumstances. We had moved to Luxembourg a few months earlier, my kids had a weeklong vacation from school and Paris—with considerably sunnier skies than dour Luxembourg—was a three-hour drive away. I told myself that I wanted to take Cai now that he was old enough to enjoy it, but the truth was that I wanted to blow Mari's mind. I wanted to shower her in princesses.

It was more like a princess monsoon. Though we'd brought along her Elsa dress to wear at the Princess Lunch, on our first Disney day we purchased the dress Mari had been begging us to buy for almost two years—the pink Aurora dress. The first time Mari asked us for this dress, we were a princess-dress-less family. Eventually Mari procured a Hello Kitty princess dress from yours truly (see chapter 2), and then an Elsa dress from Matt's parents. I never said no to the Aurora dress. I just said, "Maybe one day we'll find it! Keep your eyes open!" Secretly I was thinking, *We will never cross paths with that dress.*

We crossed paths with it about thirty seconds after entering the park on Main Street. Mari put it on immediately and didn't take it off during our four days at Disney. She wasn't the only one, either. Just a few years earlier, the little girls at Disneyland Paris were dressed in regular clothes and only changed into their gowns to go to the Princess Lunch. Now the park was peppered with small princesses, Elsas and Belles and Snow Whites. They skipped around in a froufrou dream, lining up to blast Buzz Lightyear lasers and soar through the air in flying Dumbos.

Mari loved her dress so much. She felt enchanted wearing it. But the weird thing is that I kind of felt it too.

When we'd gone to Disney with three-year-old Cai, I was a different person. All I could see was the bad food, the long lines and the incessant, overwhelming commercialization. It was one of those points on which my sister and I disagreed. I mentioned my sister in chapter 1. She and I are very close. In some ways we're similar, while in others we seem not to be related at all. *She* was into princesses as a little girl, for example, whereas I had little interest in them. Now as an adult she's still gaga for Disney. She took her kids to Disney World in Florida once a year and only stopped when she absolutely couldn't pretend they were children anymore because of their facial hair and college attendance. Whereas I look at Disney and see a corporation plotting how to make the next million dollars, she looks at Disney and sees magic.

Back to the Princess Lunch, where the Little Princesses no longer had to change into their gowns as they had in 2011, because by 2015 it had become acceptable Disney daywear. Why did this change happen?

If you're interested in the subject of Little Princesses, you might have read *Cinderella Ate My Daughter* by Peggy Orenstein, a compelling book about the way pink and princesses are marketed to young girls and an exploration of why that's happening, along with the implications of it all. The most famous revelation of the book—as mentioned in the Disney Princess Dollar Timeline—is that in 2000 a Disney executive went to a Disney on Ice show and observed little girls dressed in homemade princess gowns *because Disney wasn't manufacturing them*. It's dizzying to think about, but there was a time, quite recently, when Disney was not producing and marketing princess products. The Disney executive changed all that. He guessed that the company was missing a moneymaking opportunity. Three billion dollars later—that's what Disney princess products generate in sales—let's agree that he guessed right.

This princess culture, then, is a relatively new phenomenon. And perhaps somewhere in between 2011 and 2015, it caught on enough that girls started to wear their gowns at Disney. Or at the shopping mall. Or at the pharmacy. That's what these Little Princesses do. You've probably seen them around.

Is this a terrible phenomenon?

I'm not sure. When Mari dresses as a princess, she's allowing herself to go to a place of fantasy. It's play. It's not always a gown, either. She often walks around with one of my mother's old shawls knotted around her neck and calls it her "cape." Anytime she made a cardboard crown at school, she wore it around as much as she possibly could. Rips were repaired with Scotch tape, and she'd don the DIY crowns until they disintegrated. What was fun for us was hearing her say, whenever we prepared to leave the house, "Wait! I forgot my cape and crown!"

Can we get back to the Princess Lunch again? I'm happy to report that this time Cai ate the expensive meal we'd purchased instead of raisins. Here's what else happened:

When the princesses entered the room, Mari cried tears of joy. When they came to our table to talk to her, she was ecstatic. I can't say that I've never seen her that happy, but I haven't seen her that happy for that many hours in a row. Even Cai, who understood that these women were actresses, enjoyed it.

Here's what else happened: At the table next to ours there were two grown men having lunch. They were wearing business suits and there were no children with them. I think they were a couple, though I'm not sure. They were either French or Belgian and they had definitely not stumbled into the Princess Lunch by accident.

They were ready with their cameras and took multiple photos with the princesses. And like my daughter, they were very, very happy.

Disneyland is filled with adults like these Princess Lunch men—grown-ups without kids who willingly spend their vacation at the park, seeking out and posing with actors dressed in Mickey Mouse and Dopey and Tigger suits. In 2011, I thought these people were insane. I could not, for the life of me, understand why anyone would do this rather than go to the beach or a lake or even a cheesy all-inclusive family hotel where all you have to do is not be completely naked as you consume complimentary blue cocktails.

In 2015 with my Little Princess in tow, I understood these Disney adults better. They were grown-up, yet they still knew how to lose themselves in fantasy. They might have had jobs and mortgages and real toolkits, but they understood how to suspend disbelief in order to enjoy a moment.

Cai, Matt and I smiled at the two lunching men—who were almost as euphoric as Mari when meeting the princesses—though not in a mean-spirited way. We smiled at how much they were enjoying the fantasy. I wished I could let myself feel that happy.

Mari's princess passion is total and pure. There's nothing in my life that I'm so enthusiastic about. I realize that I'm forty-five, but I'm pretty sure I felt the same way, more or less, when I was a girl. I was an early cynic, either dismissing feminine fads or simply not understanding them. I recall having some Hello Kitty stickers in my possession when I was in grade school and not quite knowing what to do with them. I liked their bubbly texture, yet the images mystified me. Who was this mouthless feline? And why was she always holding a cherry? I never liked the color pink—not for one day of my life. But neither did I particularly love any other color. "What's your favorite color?"

people would ask me, because that's considered a good icebreaker with kids. My answer would be something along the lines of "Blue? Green? I'm not sure. Is *The Love Boat* on?"

"The problem with being from New York," I told Cai at one point during the Princess Lunch, "is that you can never really enjoy anything."[12]

When Mari fell for princesses, I started out trying to change her. As I opened myself up to the magic inside the Auberge—which I once viewed in the most cynical possible terms—I realized how much my Little Princess was actually changing me. I wasn't giddy like the men at the next table. But I was feeling the magic too.

Opposite of Serious:
FEMTASTIC FAIRY GODMOTHER AND
THE LITTLE MERMAID

Guess who's back?

When we last left Femmie, she'd fixed Sleeping Beauty *with a couple of waves of her progressive magic wand. Now our heroine takes on* The Little Mermaid, *which is in dire need of some updating. Are you ready? Hold on to your hats! And your sexy seashell bra!*

✦ ✦ ✦

Old *Little Mermaid*: Once upon a time, Ariel, a sixteen-year-old mermaid princess, was dissatisfied with her underwater life and yearned to explore the human world.

---

12 I'm from the suburbs of New York City, which means we had all of the cynicism of that city without any of the convenience of twenty-four-hour bodegas.

Femtastic *Little Mermaid*: Once upon a time, Ariel, a sixteen-year-old mermaid princess, was dissatisfied with her underwater life, so she studied anthropology and had an interesting and varied career exploring the ways human beings behave, interact and evolve.

✦ ✦ ✦

Old *Little Mermaid*: Once upon a time, Prince Eric fell in love with a mermaid named Ariel who sang to him and he was so enamored of her voice that he was tricked into falling in love with Vanessa, aka the evil Ursula, after she stole Ariel's voice.

Femtastic *Little Mermaid*: Once upon a time, a woman with a beautiful voice got laryngitis. When she realized that her boyfriend hated her a little bit each time she got sick, she took care of her voice by practicing breathing techniques and drinking lots of fluids, and then she took care of herself by dumping him.

✦ ✦ ✦

Old *Little Mermaid*: Once upon a time, yet another aging powerful woman preyed on a young, pretty innocent one.

Femtastic *Little Mermaid*: Once upon a time, Ursula decided that now she was middle-aged she didn't have time for bullshit anymore and shifted her focus onto more meaningful things and let everyone else live their lives as long as they didn't get in her face.

✦ ✦ ✦

Old *Little Mermaid*: Once upon a time, a young woman was forced to choose between the world of her father and the world of her husband.

Femtastic *Little Mermaid*: Once upon a time, a young woman had lots of choices, many of them having nothing at all to do with men. That is all.

✦ ✦ ✦

Old *Little Mermaid*: Once upon a time, Ariel gave up her voice so that she could chase some guy she met and liked.

Femtastic *Little Mermaid*: Once upon a time, Ariel was about to give up her voice to chase a man she barely knew, but then her father told her that she was perfect just as she was and that any man worthy of her would figure that out. She believed him. And they all lived happily ever after.

My Life in Pink:
THE NEON PINK FORCE AWAKENS

Something amazing happened! Mari became interested in something that has nothing whatsoever to do with pink or princesses! I mean—almost nothing to do with princesses. There is one princess involved, but it's okay because she's actually the secret child of the Dark Sith Lord Vader and she's also a powerful rebel leader and a future general.

How did this happy event happen?

Because of Cai, of course. Just as Mari became attached to Disney princesses without ever having seen a Disney princess movie, so too Cai became a fan of *Star Wars* long before he ever saw the films. And though they pretend to be bitter enemies, my children secretly love each other and Mari absorbed the *Star Wars* passion from her older brother.

Thrilled that not one character in any of the films ever wears hot pink, I immediately capitalized on this intergalactic interest.

"Princess Leia was played by Carrie Fisher!" I told Mari. "She was so smart and funny and also a great writer! When people asked her about losing weight to play Leia in the new *Star Wars* film, she told them the subject was stupid. She . . . Hey, wake up!"

It turned out that Mari wasn't all that interested in Carrie Fisher's challenge to the Hollywood establishment, which expects women to have the decency not to age. She liked *Star Wars* because her brother liked it, because the story of good vs. evil spoke to her and because the costumes appealed to her love of pageantry.

And yet, getting away from Disney is not so easily accomplished, unless you've just gone ahead and become an anti-pop-culture hermit living off the grid. In 2012, Disney bought the *Star Wars* franchise. It also bought Marvel Entertainment in 2009, which is now exploding as a brand (in a good way) thanks to new Netflix series like *Luke Cage*.

Though Disney was still pulling the money puppet strings, Matt and I decided to encourage Mari's interest in *Star Wars*, because at least it wasn't princesses. So when *The Force Awakens* came out, we decided to catch up on the culture. We watched all the previous films with the kids with the intention of seeing the new episode together in the movie theater.[13] Episodes 4, 5 and 6 were fun but 1, 2 and 3 were way too scary. As parents, we were not at our best when showing these films to our kids. We came to our senses only shortly before the end of episode 3 and stopped the film before the gruesome end. The kids still slept terribly that night.

We put our plans to see *The Force Awakens* on hold, and the next time the kids asked us to watch a movie, Matt and I were determined to show them the happiest, least scary film ever made. Interestingly, it's *Singin' in the Rain*, which stars Debbie Reynolds, who was the mother of Carrie Fisher.[14] But sadly, after watching *Star Wars* my kids had no interest in *Singin' in the Rain*.

Thanks a lot, George Lucas.

✦ ✦ ✦

---

13 When Cai was four we would never have shown him such scary films, but Mari is a second child who was duly neglected.

14 The two women died one day apart while I wrote this book. It was a sad time for all princesses.

Interesting Little Princess Fact #5

Disney Collector is a young Brazilian woman named Melissa Lima with 8 million YouTube subscribers.[15] Is it just me, or does she seem more sincere than the other "unboxers" selling crap to toddlers on YouTube? It's like the other ones are just phoning it in and don't really enjoy playing with MagiClip dolls in the bathtub. Disney Collector is definitely feeling it, though, as if she really wants to send Petal Float Ariel down the slide of the Water Palace playset. Know what I mean?

✦ ✦ ✦

Little Princess Pie

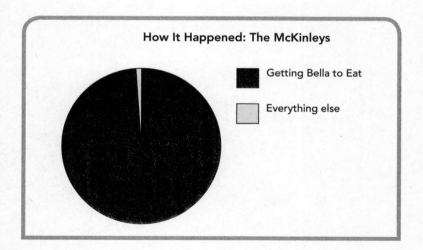

---

15 Or at least she told the *New York Times* that her name is Melissa Lima. But she still remains an enigma wrapped in an immaculate Hello Kitty manicure.

Little Bella was born premature, weighing in at just 5.1 pounds. She was jaundiced and had difficulty latching on to her mother's breast. Each time she was weighed, her parents waited for the results with tears in their eyes, praying that she'd gained.

Bella is two and a half now and absolutely fine, but that hasn't registered with her parents, who have never emerged from their "must feed Bella" vortex. Which is why Bella is a Little Princess who easily negotiates for a new Barbie doll each time she agrees to eat a hot dog.

PART 2

The Little Princess Outside Our Home

Now that we understand what a Little Princess is, which parent is buying her pink toilet rim blocks, and why fashion magazines are the new poison apples, let's step outside our homes. I hope we don't meet up with any big, bad wolves.

Hey, it's pretty nice out here! I can smell the wet earth and there's a squirrel scampering up a maple tree. I should definitely get outside more often.

Wait, what's that? There *are* wolves hiding around here somewhere? Just around the corner there are pitfalls, which are all colluding against our Little Princesses' ability to reach their potential?

There are, but never fear. Since we've established that you can indeed learn something from the princesses, let's have a look at the perils that lie ahead, and let's enlist the help of one of the princesses to address them. Because our Little Princesses aren't going to be little forever, and we'd do well to understand what's coming. So grab the keys to your pumpkin carriages and let's go.

Chapter 6

REAL PRINCESSES AREN'T PASSIVE CREAM PUFFS

My Life in Pink:
THE *FROZEN* FILES,
PART 2—WHY ELSA REALLY RAN

Conceal, don't feel, don't let them know. Well, now they know.

—Elsa

Women are the weaker sex. We have a difficult time opening doors all by ourselves and we faint when we see mice. That's why for so many years most people thought we couldn't be a POTUS. And some people still believe that![1]

Sadly, Little Princesses don't know any of that. They think they can do anything they want and have everything they want.

---

1 Google "why a woman should not be president" and see how many people genuinely believe it. Then cry.

They even go through an adorable stage where if they don't do and get all that stuff, they make your life hell.

When people critique the Sleepy Trio of Cinderella, Snow White and Sleeping Beauty, one of the princess character traits that is most scorned is passivity. These ladies aren't active participants in their own lives. They wait around—sometimes in eternal sleep or in a deathlike coma—for someone to save them.[2]

And since these films appeal to little girls, we parents fear that our daughters will absorb the message that they should be docile to get the good things in life.

Excuse me. I have to go laugh uncontrollably for a moment. Talk amongst yourselves.

Phew. I'm back. *(Wiping away tears.)* It's so good to laugh!

Most people with Little Princesses would be hard-pressed to use the word "passive" in the same sentence as their child's name. Mari, for example, is *not* passive. She's pure impulse. She's a jumble of wants and needs and affection and demands and joy and sadness and spontaneity and love and volatile mood swings all wrapped up in an adorable fuchsia package.

Mari is free and in touch with her needs and wants and desires—so much so that she steamrolled her way into a princess culture her mother despised. But cryptically, instead of trying to emulate her, I'm constantly reining her in. If she demands treats, I say no. If she wants to watch Disney Collector at five a.m., I tell her she can't. When she asks for a new dress, I point out that she has more dresses than I do even though I've had four more decades of shopping opportunities than she has. I spend consider-

---

2 Although if any of these characters had actually been mothers, I think we might have forgiven them all that sleep.

able time trying to get her to not draw on the couch with markers, to put on clothing, to eat, to stop hitting her brother, to not use her chalks on the couch, to walk rather than be carried, to leave the house, to return to the house, to get into the bath and pajamas and go to sleep instead of painting the couch—all activities she resists with varying degrees of intensity.

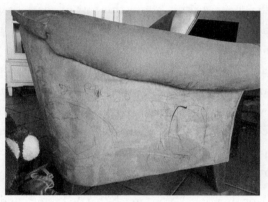

Our couch.
(Photo Credit: Mother seeking new couch in 2021)

Having spent years in a state of depression, I think about what led to it, what sustained it and what was going on inside my head. I mentioned in the first chapter that a passive approach to life, in which you imagine something outside yourself—like, say, a prince—can come along and save you, is correlated with depression. But passivity was just one aspect of my depressive way of thinking. I was also afraid of emotions and rejected my own.

One theory of depression suggests that repressed emotions and desires are at the root. We're taught at a young age that anger is bad. So are greed, selfishness and—unless your parents were like my friend Roger's[3]—sexual desire. Girls additionally get the message that being assertive is bad, as is being too smart or adventurous or strong. Even being sad is frowned upon. We are meant to be cheery in order not to inconvenience others, whether we're at the office or walking down the street or discussing national security.[4] By the time we reach adolescence, many of us are silent, afraid, deeply insecure and lost.

Much has been written about this loss of spark that happens to girls. In *The Second Sex*, Simone de Beauvoir wrote about how girls are not born "feminine" but are socialized into accepting passivity and dependence as they become the "object" of men rather than the "subject" of their own lives, meaning a person with her own needs and desires. Mary Pipher, a clinical psychologist, wrote extensively about adolescent girls in *Reviving Ophelia*. While exploring the lives of her teenage patients, she observed this common thread:

> Girls stop thinking, "Who am I? What do I want?" and start thinking, "What must I do to please others?"

I remember the exact moment when I did that. In elementary school I was a loudmouthed kid. Teachers told my parents I'd grow up to become a lawyer because I always talked back and made a fuss when something was unfair, making a case on my own behalf or on behalf of my class. I wasn't pretty, nor was I

---

3 Roger and his three brothers grew up in a home in which there was a jar of condoms on his parents' dresser. He's the only person I know who's had an uncomplicated, fulfilling and satisfying sex life. Are those two facts causal or coincidental? I'm not really asking that question. The answer is obvious unless you fear sex and sexuality, which many of us do.

4 When discussing national security during her presidential campaign, Hillary Clinton was critiqued for not smiling. It wasn't the first time she was told she should smile.

feminine. Clothes didn't interest me. There were always knots in my frizzy hair. I never fantasized that I'd become Miss America.[5]

Just before I started junior high—the seventh grade in those days—I changed. This was a conscious decision. I recall telling myself, *I'm going to change now.* Instead of being the girl who always spoke up, I told myself I'd be quiet.

It's so weird to think back on that now. I actually chose to become someone else, someone that bore little relation to the person I'd been. Boys were no doubt on my mind. Without telling myself it was so, I suspected that boys might not like me if I was too loud.

In the end, boys didn't like me anyway, which sucked for me because just a few years later I was sex obsessed. I thought about sex night and day, at cheerleading practice and at the drive-in and while hanging out with my girlfriends on the bleachers.[6] I didn't share that desire with anyone, though—not verbally and certainly not physically. Sex was a colossal and complicated and shameful secret. My desires were kept hidden and I never told a soul.

Nor did I share other desires. For years I never talked about wanting to become a writer. I believed it was frivolous and narcissistic and deep down I feared I'd fail. I wrote in secret, which is pretty nuts. In general I believed emotions and desires

---

5 It was around that time that I wrote my sixth grade school report on Denmark. You were probably wondering whatever happened with that, so here are some highlights: Denmark is a country in northern Europe that is part of Scandinavia. Copenhagen is the capital of Denmark. The country is 26,364 square miles in size. Its famous pastry is traditionally topped with icing. I'm foreshadowing something here. Bear with me.

6 None of that is true except for the sex obsession. When you grow up in a religious school where there are no cheerleaders or dances or school plays, you're forever convinced that kids in other schools are having much more fun than you are. So I just borrowed all of that from *Grease.*

of any kind were bad and shameful. I buried myself so deeply that by the time I entered college I was veiled in virtual darkness, ready to spend my young adulthood in a state of depression. And I don't want to brag, but I totally nailed it!

On a completely unrelated note, why did Elsa really run away?

Before we ever watched it, I was ready to hate *Frozen*. It's a princess movie. It's a musical. It introduced a song that everyone was singing regardless of their particular vocal talents. What's not to hate?

Frozen was released when Mari was two years old. She was too young to know about it or even ask to see it. I probably could have avoided princess movies for another few years. But when she turned three, I saw the film was coming on our cable package and spontaneously recorded it on our DVR. Matt and Cai had started to watch movies together and I thought it would be fun to make popcorn and watch a flick with my daughter.

Once Anna knocked on Elsa's door to ask her to build that snowman, I was hooked. I loved the characters and the setup—the once close sisters whose relationship was damaged by a secret. As the plot unfolded I loved it even more, exactly the same way Olaf felt about his nose when Anna thumped the carrot through his head.

What I connected to most about this movie, however, was Elsa—the girl who was told to fear her own magic. Elsa was born with a talent, an expression, a quality unique to her. She was taught to be afraid of it. She was persuaded to repress what made her special, so much so that she shut off from the people she loved and from the rest of the world.

I used to tell Mari that Elsa ran away to the mountains because she was afraid of hurting the people she loved. That's only partially true. The full story is that after spending her life repressing and self-negating—doing the exact dance that adolescent girls are taught to do—Elsa was forced in an unguarded moment to express her true self. When she finally did, she was met with fear, shaming and hostility. And she took off.

Why did Elsa *really* run away? Because she was finished pleasing others. She didn't want to hide her true self anymore.

Princess Studies 101:
YES AND NO

In its most harmless forms, women's and girls' propensity to accommodate others rather than themselves can result in getting into a conversation you have no desire to engage in, working overtime without pay or reluctantly baking cupcakes for some event, like, say, a bridal shower.

Episodes like these deplete a woman over time—because they're always doing for others and not taking care of their own needs—but the tendency to accommodate others is profoundly damaging in sexual situations. I'm lucky because I was never sexually assaulted (one in five women are), though as a teenager I was groped and kissed without consent because I couldn't bring myself to say no. It's so simple a word and yet I couldn't access it. I was unprepared, embarrassed, and didn't have the tools or language to deal with the situation.

When you read women's accounts of having nonconsensual sex that they don't call rape or sexual assault—because they blame themselves for not being more assertive about saying no—is it sexual assault? American law is confusing on this subject because each state has varying laws and definitions. "Consent" is defined differently according to each state, including whether silence indicates a lack of consent, or whether a person has to say no before it's considered assault.[7]

Meanwhile, as I was researching the female tendency not to say no—and I'll get to some of those studies soon—I came across a disturbing trend. When I did an initial online search for why women might say yes when they mean no, here are the types of links that came up:

- 5 Reasons "No" Might Mean "Yes" (MarieClaire.com)

- 7 Reasons Why Women Say No When They Mean Yes (King Kurtis Smith's Life Transforming Blog)

- 17 Things Women Say and What They Really Mean (Mensxp.com)

- When Women Say No Do They Really Mean It? (Pointless Online Forum)

- Why is it, when women say no, they really mean yes? (Quora)

I could cry reading these titles. I live in a little bubble with a partner who hears "no" and understands the meaning of the word. Yet outside my home there's often an assumption that when women *do* say no, they don't mean it. There's a culture that undermines girls and women by not believing what they say, by doubting their honesty and their ability to know and understand themselves. It's absolutely horrible.

And yes, on top of this bullshit, plenty of women have a hard

---

7 If you or anyone you know is confused about consent, search "Tea Consent" on YouTube or go to www.consentiseverything.com.

time saying no. A 2013 study found that women volunteer more frequently at work and are asked to volunteer more frequently for "non-promotable tasks."[8] A 2014 study from the Society for Industrial and Organizational Psychology found that women are more likely to say yes to excessive workplace requests.[9]

"Women typically are regarded as nurturers and helpers, so saying 'no' runs against the grain of what might be expected of them," said Baylor School of Medicine researcher Katharine O'Brien, who has conducted three studies on the differences between men and women in their ability to say no to work requests. "Women feel a stronger sense of guilt when they say 'no' and feel bad when they do. In addition, they do not want to be denigrated by managers and coworkers. Those are powerful reasons why women are more likely to agree to extra work."

There are also powerful reasons why women stay silent in sexual situations. When women are sexually coerced—asked again and again, made to feel guilty or obligated, or pressured into sex using other forms of emotional and psychological coercion—they often stay silent.

Some people would define the groping incident I described earlier as assault. He was fourteen, I was thirteen and it didn't get very far. It wasn't assault but it *was* a case of two teenagers who had never been taught to talk about sex.

I considered leaving a section about sexual assault out of this

---

8 L. Vesterlund et al., "Breaking the glass ceiling with 'no': Gender differences in declining requests for non-promotable tasks," Carnegie Mellon Working Paper (2013).

9 Katharine O'Brien et al., "Women find it more difficult to say 'no' to executive workplace requests," *Society for Industrial and Organizational Psychology* (2014).

book for the very reason I have included it in the end. Talking both about sex and about sexual assault makes people feel embarrassed and uncomfortable and ashamed.

What if it didn't? Can we raise children to talk about sex and listen openly to discussions about sex and consent? Can we educate our children—both boys and girls—about sexual assault and how not to be a perpetrator, and also how to try to protect themselves against being a victim? Can we explicitly teach our children that assault is never the fault of the victim? And can we separate shame from everything that surrounds the subject of sex?

And what is all this doing in a book about Little Princesses?

If I want to encourage my daughter to express who she truly is, that must absolutely include however she feels about her body and sex. If we're talking about the freedom to express yourself, sex should be at the top of the list because it's the very subject traditionally denied to women. I'm encouraged by the sex-positive movement, which embraces all sexual choices as positive, including promiscuity and abstinence and everything in between as long as there is explicit consent and safety.

I have a few years before I'll discuss any of this with Mari, though we're already talking to Cai about how people feel ashamed of sex, about how people judge and oppress gay and trans people, and about other issues surrounding the subject of sex. The technicalities of the birds and the bees can wait, but if I possibly can, I want to raise children who will be more comfortable in their sexual skin than I was. I want them to be aware of the concept and need for enthusiastic consent, and to feel free to be themselves.

Opposite of Serious:
SNOW WHITE GETS A FEMTASTIC MAKEOVER

Hooray! Femtastic Fairy Godmother is back and she's ready to take on Snow White. *Snow has been around longer than any other Disney princess, so her story is definitely ready for some updating.*

Hi there, and hello!

✦ ✦ ✦

Old *Snow White*: Once upon a time, a queen wanted to be the fairest in the land.

If I had a magic mirror, I'd ask, "Is there really free will? Or are we just puppets like Pinocchio?"

Femtastic *Snow White*: Once upon a time, a queen wanted to be the fairest in the land and then Snow White shaved her hair in an effort to show the queen how silly all of this beauty stuff really was. The queen had a good laugh and they went out for a drink together.

◆ ◆ ◆

Old *Snow White*: Once upon a time, a queen wanted to be the fairest in the land.

If you Google "mirror on the wall," a Lil Wayne song is the first result that comes up. That must drive the Evil Queen crazy.

Femtastic *Snow White*: Once upon a time, a queen wanted to be the fairest in the land and then asked herself, "Really? Is that really what I want?" Then she realized that what she actually wanted was love, so she adopted a puppy.

◆ ◆ ◆

Old *Snow White*: Once upon a time, a queen wanted to be the fairest in the land.

In the Brothers Grimm version, the Evil Queen's punishment is having to go to a bridal shower. Ha ha—just kidding! But she did have to go to a wedding in hot iron shoes and dance herself to death.

Femtastic *Snow White*: Once upon a time, a queen wanted to be the fairest in the land, so she became a fitness guru and built an empire based on workout videos. Oh, wait. That was Jane Fonda.

✦ ✦ ✦

Old *Snow White*: Once upon a time, a queen wanted to be the fairest in the land.

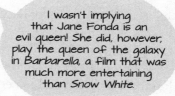

I wasn't implying that Jane Fonda is an evil queen! She did, however, play the queen of the galaxy in *Barbarella*, a film that was much more entertaining than *Snow White*.

Femtastic *Snow White*: Once upon a time, a queen wanted to be the fairest in the land, so she raised taxes on the wealthy, made higher education free for all, instituted paid family leave, expanded health care and supported people living in poverty. Everyone agreed she was the fairest in the land.

✦ ✦ ✦

Old *Snow White*: Once upon a time, a queen wanted to be the fairest in the land.

People have always feared powerful women. In the olden days, they burned them as witches. Now they're called "bitches" and "shrill" and "untrustworthy."

Femtastic *Snow White*: Once upon a time, a woman wanted to be president. She didn't make it. Not all fairy tales have a happy ending.

My Life in Pink: THE *FROZEN* FILES, PART 3— WHY ELSA SANG

> No right, no wrong, no rules for me. I'm free!
>
> —Elsa

I've watched *Frozen* with Mari at least half a dozen times. I eventually learned it by heart, and sometimes I'd observe Mari instead, which was a fun show in a different way. As Mari watched the movie, she always had a sweet, unconscious smile on her face. She especially lit up during the songs, and she was most excited when Elsa began singing "Let It Go."

So was I. I can't watch that scene without tearing up. Those tears—and the emotions that lie behind them—are going to help me raise my Little Princess. I'll explain why, but first, I wanted to share this handy Primer for Depression. Since I spent so many years in one, I've outlined what helped me sustain a viable, long-term lugubrious funk. If you're interested in becoming depressed, I do hope these instructions can work for you.[10]

1. Whatever you need is wrong. Reject it.

2. Whatever you want is wrong. Reject it.

3. Whatever you feel is wrong. Reject it.

---

10 You're welcome!

4. Identify your flaws. You thought I was going to say, "Reject them," right? Ha-ha-ha, of course not! *Focus* on your flaws. They are an important part of your depression.

5. Identify the flaws of others and dwell on them as well. When you're in a relationship, this is especially functional in order to nurture depression. But even if you're single, use the flaws of others to bolster the claim that the world is a bad place and also to remain alone.

6. Cultivate negative thoughts and allow them to convince you that life is terrible, that you are a victim and that everything is hopeless. Believe your thoughts. Believe the ones that pop into your head, but also the ones that stay in your mind and occupy you for days and weeks and months at a time. Believe the thoughts that cause you to feel anxiety and fear, the ones that keep you awake at night and the ones that keep you isolated from other people. Honor this axiom: You *are* your thoughts. If your thoughts are sad, then you *are* sadness. There is no truth other than your thoughts . . .

7. . . . And your emotions. You are also your emotions. If you feel anger, then that's who you are. Same with pain or fear or shame or any of the other really fun ones.

8. When something happens, resist it by thinking, "I wish this wasn't happening," or, "Why is this happening?" When you do this properly, your body should resist and clench as well, causing headaches, stomach problems and other tension-related illnesses. Ailments are always helpful in sustaining depression.

9. Under no circumstances should you accept yourself. Ever. Particularly with all those flaws you've identified.

10. Do your very best to not get enough sleep. This can be best accomplished by focusing on anxiety-producing thoughts, and also by drinking too much booze or late-night coffee. Drugs are also fab.

11. Stay isolated from other people, which should be a cinch by now. Some people are your enemies. But even the ones who aren't will hurt you in the end.

In my early thirties I emerged from depression with the help of medication. It was amazing. I recall feeling my mind clearing. I recognized thoughts of optimism and joy that I had not had for years. There were some problems, though. I was in a dysfunctional relationship with a dysfunctional man, for example.[11] We both went into therapy, which helped us individually and as a couple, and a few years later Matt raised the possibility of having a baby. Ahead of starting to try to conceive, I went off antidepressants.

As I mentioned in chapter 2, I was fearful that depression would return if I had a baby. But by then something important had changed. I had learned a few skills.

I'd started exercising regularly, for example. While not a panacea for depression, exercise helps. And about a year before I conceived, I'd taken a course in mindfulness and meditation. Here are some things you learn when you practice mindfulness and meditation:

1. Whatever you need is okay. Accept it. Even if you don't get everything you need, accept that feeling of need.

2. Whatever you want is okay. Accept it. Even if you don't get everything you want, accept that you want it.

---

11 If you recall, Matt and I were both a bit of a fixer-upper.

3. Whatever you feel is *definitely* okay. Accept it and welcome it.

4. Identify your flaws and weaknesses and accept them. While you're at it, identify your good qualities and accept them too.

5. Accept the flaws and weaknesses of the people around you. Identify their good qualities and gifts to you and feel gratitude.

6. Cultivate positive thoughts whenever possible. When you feel that life is terrible, that you are a victim and that everything is hopeless, don't judge yourself for feeling this way, but also ask yourself, "Is it really true?" Acknowledge all the thoughts that pop into your mind. Observe them. Some of them are true and some are not. Just watch them come and go. The ones that make you feel anxiety and fear and shame are often deceptive. When the thoughts keep you up at night, watch them, laugh at them if you can and choose a different focus. Like the breath. Or gratitude. Or love. Or just think about a puppy. In any event, like everything else, the anxious thoughts will pass. Everything passes.

7. You are not your thoughts or your emotions. There is a being, an energy, a soul, a whatever you would like to call it, inside you that is separate from your thoughts and emotions. It is the root of you, always there, as all the small and big things pass.

8. When something happens, accept it. This doesn't mean you cannot try to change the world for the better, because we definitely need more of that. It does mean that at any given moment, you can accept your life the way it is.

9. Accept yourself. Accept yourself. Accept yourself. Wants, needs, desires, strengths, weaknesses, talents, flaws, vulnerabilities, the good, the bad and the ugly, vermicelli hair—every single thing.

10. Breathe. Let your body relax. When you do this enough, you sleep more easily and more deeply. Breathing can also help you access the energy/spirit/whatever-you-would-like-to-call-it, and this has the potential to give you strength and balance and resilience.

11. We're all in this together. Let's cultivate the feeling of compassion that makes us aware that we are One. Whoever you see as "the other," consider that you and that person are connected.

Taking a course like this doesn't have the same effect as pixie dust. I didn't magically transform after eight weeks of meditating and practicing mindfulness. I did learn some skills, however. One was learning how to accept myself. I don't accept myself every hour of every day, though I can recognize when I'm not and I know how to try. Neither do I surrender to every moment, but at least I know how. It's a skill I'd lost long ago in childhood and now I can manage it sometimes. When I surrender it's peaceful and wonderful and feels like coming home. Other times it's chaotic and confusing and painful. But surrender is still better than resisting.

The "Let It Go" scene, in which Elsa sings that song and builds the ice palace, is already a classic cinematic moment, though the movie is even younger than Mari. The beauty of the sequence, which begins when Elsa takes off her glove and lets her magic flow from her hands, isn't from the song. The power lies in what's happening to the character and the change she's undergoing. When she was a little girl, Elsa buried a part of herself. It happens to be the vital part of her, the part that is at once most special and also the one other people fear, judge and hate.

When she's finally alone in the mountains outside of Arendelle, Elsa releases what she has repressed. Apart from society, from its judgments, from its expectations and its burdens, Elsa becomes her true self for the first time since childhood. She's fearless, and this fearlessness makes her joyful, beautiful and creative. She builds something that matches her now unconstrained soul. She even breathes life into an adorable snowman.

Did I mention that I liked this movie?

No one ever warned me that I'd go through a stage when I'd feel compelled to give up a part of myself or that I might need some skills to get it back. It's okay that my parents never told me—no one told them, either. I was lucky enough to find a toolkit and I will try to pass it on to my daughter, and to my son, for that matter. This book is about Little Princesses, but boys lose their spark too. They need our help just as much as girls.

When she was three years old, Mari used to put on her cape and tiara, stand in front of the mirror, pretend to let her nonexistent braid down and belt out the following:

"Let it go. Let it go. I can't hominom anymore."

She'd do this at home and also outdoors, in front of the mirrors at H&M, in elevators and parking lots—anywhere the mood struck her, really. Like so many kids, she'd just start singing when she felt joyful. She still does, because she's in touch with what she feels and can express without repression. I try to give Mari the message that what she wants is okay, even if she doesn't always get it. I say no to constant candy, but if Mari asks to wear her tutu every day, I say yes. We have consequently had entire weeks of tutu wearing.[12]

But in just a few years, Mari—and all the Little Princesses— will reach adolescence. The process of becoming a woman will teach Mari that her wants and needs don't matter, and that she

---

12 My rule was, if there was no poop on the tutu, she could wear it.

should instead invest her energies on looking pretty, fitting in, pleasing others and not offending. Even if I'm the perfect parent, and I'm not,[13] people and society and shampoo commercials will come along and spoil all her freewheelin' fun. Misogyny—which still rears its ugly head—will also try to bury her spirit. She'll be encouraged to repress rather than express, to keep her head down and stay quiet for fear of shining.

And here's the fun part. If I want to teach Mari about what happens to girls when they hide their true selves, and what glorious things occur when they express the very things they were taught to hide, I can now *actually reference a princess.*

For someone who grew up with the Sleepy Trio, that's a wonderful, if ironic, surprise. Instead of Cinderella and Snow White and Sleeping Beauty, who stayed quiet and asleep and passive, Mari was born just in time to have a heroine worthy of her.

I don't need Mari to be successful or to get married or to be or an ice palace architect or anything like that. What I want for her, more than anything else, is to not get shut down for as long as I did. I think the shutdown happens to most people in adolescence. But it doesn't last over a decade for everyone.

"Look at Elsa," I can tell Mari. "She gave up the most important part of herself. But then she got it back."

Real Princesses aren't passive cream puffs after all.

I can't say that I'm never passive anymore, or that I'm authentic all the time. I'm trying, though, for myself and so that I can be a better role model for my kids. And every time I notice myself hiding, burying a truth, letting fear overtake me or repressing

---

13 Here's a list of what I do perfectly: finding travel deals, choosing desserts and writing down passwords in places where I can find them. Mic drop, bitches.

what I feel, I know just what to do: stand in front of the mirror and pretend to let down my braid. Then say:

"Let it go. Let it go. I can't hominom anymore."

✦ ✦ ✦

Interesting Little Princess Fact #6

Just because I'm opening up to princesses, this doesn't mean the way the toy industry is unfolding is okay. When toys are marketed specifically to boys or to girls, it's dumb and limiting. Parents know that, and there are movements to stop the gender segregation of toys. In 2015, Target decided to stop labeling toys and bedding with "Girls" and "Boys" signs. Hopefully Toys "R" Us and others will follow suit.

✦ ✦ ✦

Little Princess Pie

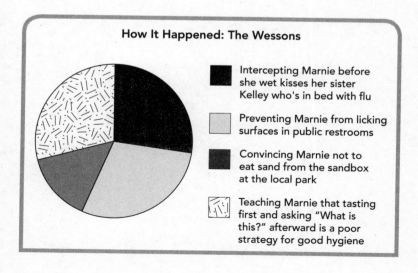

How It Happened: The Wessons

Intercepting Marnie before she wet kisses her sister Kelley who's in bed with flu

Preventing Marnie from licking surfaces in public restrooms

Convincing Marnie not to eat sand from the sandbox at the local park

Teaching Marnie that tasting first and asking "What is this?" afterward is a poor strategy for good hygiene

Marnie's mother is a pediatrician, which comes in handy, though it also presents a certain irony as Marnie refuses to accept that germs are really a thing. Once in a while her parents see the humor of Marnie's heedless ways, but mostly they're exhausted by her constant challenges to hygienic common sense. Like all the other Little Princess parents, the Wessons have zero energy left for princess resistance.

While she loves all the princesses, Marnie feels a special kinship with Snow White for eating a poisonous apple given to her by a dubious, sinister stranger. When Marnie's parents took her to eat a special lunch with the princesses at Disney World, Marnie tried to lick Ariel's hand and wipe her nose on Cinderella's sleeve. They have not returned.

Chapter 7

REAL WOMEN DON'T CACKLE

My Life in Pink:
CACKLING SISTERS VS. ANNA AND ELSA

Picture this:

Once upon a time, on a rainy Sunday, there were two bored children who didn't much like long car rides and two parents desperately trying to figure out what to do with them. Everyone tossed around a few lame ideas, and then the father said, "Why don't we go to a movie?"

This scintillating tale is based on a true story. Yes—it was us! And though a movie might seem like the obvious choice, Matt and I had yet to take the kids to see one in the theater, mostly because after we'd become parents we'd gotten out of the habit of going ourselves. We'd gotten out of the habit of going out at all, but don't play the violins because Matt and I like being at home. That's the way it is with introverts. Going out is exhausting. Even the thought of going out is exhausting. The truth is that we had kids so that we could have an excuse for why we couldn't go out anymore. It was a brilliant strategy.

On the Sunday in question we checked the listings. We were living in Jerusalem at the time and the only children's movie that was playing in English was Disney's live-action version of *Cinderella*.

One small detail made this dreary prospect exciting. We'd get to see Anna and Elsa again. Disney had made a short film called *Frozen Fever*, which was screening before *Cinderella*. Which meant that if the legions of *Frozen*-obsessed little girls wanted to see the new *Frozen* film, they *had* to see the new *Cinderella*. It was also a brilliant strategy.

"I don't want to see *Cinderella*," Cai said wisely. I was with him on this one. On the other hand, I thought, my Little Princess was opening me up to new ideas. *Maybe it will be fun,* I told myself.

"Let's watch the trailer and then decide," I suggested.

Trailers are that thing where moviemakers stuff the best moments of a film into three dazzling minutes while schmaltzy melodramatic music makes you cry and the whole experience of watching it causes you to think, "I will die if I do not see this movie."

In that sense, the *Cinderella* trailer didn't succeed, because instead it caused me to think, "I would rather plan and attend a dozen bridal showers and then edit the bridal shower videos with 'My Heart Will Go On' as the soundtrack in a constant loop. I would rather listen to some dummy explain to me why poor people are responsible for their misfortune. I would rather stand in line at the post office. Anything at all. Just please don't ever make me watch this movie."

The trailer was beyond awful. And since even bad movies

sometimes have good trailers, I had to conclude that the actual film was even worse. I could be wrong about this. I can't imagine ever earmarking the two hours to find out, however.

Why was the trailer so excruciating? It wasn't the plot. It's *fine* that at the heart of this film lies a love story. While they aren't my favorite movies, even with all my cynicism I would never expect Disney to tinker with the premise that Cinderella is about a prince and a down-on-her-luck woman falling in love.

What offended me about the trailer was its portrayal of women. The problem with this film isn't the "man saves woman" plot. It's the way the film pits women against each other. The cackling stepsisters are so cruel they make Hannibal Lecter seem sympathetic. The way the sisters hate Cinderella—in the trailer they mock and denigrate her and tear her dress, for heaven's sake—is disturbing. The stepmother, who is supposed to take care of Cinderella, is hateful.

In real life, women *are* victimized by other women. Sometimes. But let's get real. Many more women are victimized by men. This is not man-hating rhetoric. It's just the way it is.[1]

Women aren't always nice to each other—as discussed in chapter 4. Our brains evolved to believe that we're competing for sperm, which is why we still look each other up and down and roll our eyes—a staple of Valley Girl culture.[2] We've all known some mean girls who forget to stop and think, "Wait a minute!

---

1 The Centers for Disease Control and Prevention estimates that approximately one in five women have been sexually assaulted in their lifetime. One in three have been sexually harassed at work.

2 For the uninitiated: Valley Girls were a thing in the 1980s. They introduced the word "like" as a quotative, as in, *I was, like, "Oh, my God, my daughter is* so *into princesses right now."*

We're not hunter-gatherers anymore! I can get sperm and be nice all at the same time!"

I've had a few female bosses and colleagues who acted as if they hated me and who tried to demean me. There are women in my life who put other women down and begrudge their successes. I know some mean girls.

But I know many, many more good ones. I'm writing this book because a group of women writers got together to help and empower each other, and because women editors and agents championed my work. All my life I've been lucky to have women friends who are nurturing, encouraging and validating. My mother is fab and my sister is truly my sister—we love each other in a very uncomplicated and pure way.[3]

Here's a graphic to illustrate the true breakdown of how women behave in real life:

---

3 It's, like, totally one of the reasons I loved *Frozen*.

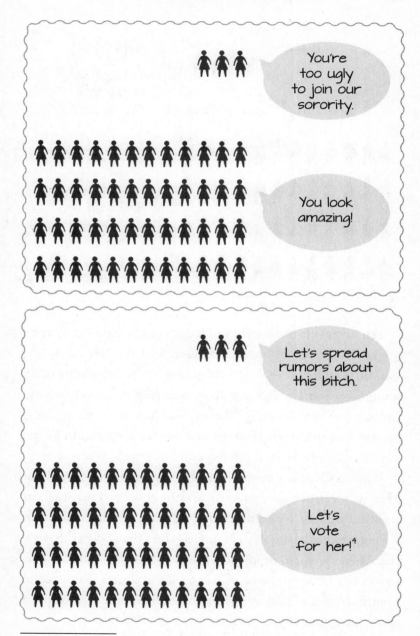

---

4 If women had been the only voters in the 2016 election, Hillary Clinton would be president. Fifty-four percent of women voted for her.

Yes, in real life we women still judge one another—in fact, it's one of the themes of Internet content. Surf the Net randomly, and you'll soon find an article about how you're doing something wrong as a woman. The way you're applying makeup is wrong. The way you date is wrong. The way you have sex is wrong, as is the way you treat your husband and mother your children. The way you age, of course, is offensive and in general you suck.

Women's hostility toward women is still a phenomenon, but when we create female characters who are either evil stepsisters or beautiful victims, we reinforce this old story of women as rivals. We perpetuate the obsolescent model rather than bolster the new one. When women are pitted against each other in the media and in the Disney remake of *Cinderella*, it does a disservice to women. In this respect at least, Disney might have figured out a more interesting way to retell the story of *Cinderella*.

Disney did manage to portray women and their relationship with each other in a positive way in a newer princess flick, and that film made a cool $3 billion.[5] The new *Cinderella* made a ton of cash too, though I would argue that many little girls were led back to the vapid ball because of the clever tie-in to the billion-dollar movie, which told a much better tale.

Frozen resonates because the heart and soul of the story is the beautiful relationship between two sisters. Many of us can relate. As I watched the movie for the first time, I got maudlin thinking about my sister thousands of miles away. I bet I'm not alone in my sisterly devotion. How many women can relate to the story of two sisters who love each other? And how many can relate to Cinderella?

Life isn't a contest between women. If love is the answer, the first place it arises from is women. Let's promote, encourage and nurture the love at the expense of that fossilized idea of sniping, backstabbing, competing women.

I don't want Mari to see the new *Cinderella* at all. If she's going to see it, however, at least we'll wait until she's old enough to have a conversation about the way the women are portrayed. I know women aren't always kind and good to each other and, as with the other obstacles in life, I hope to give Mari the tools to deal with meanness when she confronts it. And I'll also remind her that the truth lies not in the cackling sisters, but in the ones who support, cherish and love each other.

---

5 It's *Frozen*, for those who have just tuned in.

Princess Studies 101:
WOMAN VS. WOMAN

Madeleine Albright said there is "a special place in hell for women who don't help each other."

She was criticized for saying it—at the time she was encouraging women to support Hillary Clinton's candidacy for president—but I bet women who have tried to climb the ladder of success were more forgiving of her dramatic admonition.

Women who seek power or professional advancement routinely face the ugly truth that women don't always help each other on their way up. This is one of the reasons why there are still so few women in leadership roles, even though we make up more than half of the workforce.

A 2016 study shed light on why women might not advance the careers of other women. Published in the *Academy of Management Journal*, the study found that women who promote diversity at work—meaning they encourage hiring and promoting women and people of color—get lower work evaluations from their bosses and colleagues.[6]

Much of the bias that holds women and minorities back is subtle. It's not as obvious as a racial slur or a misogynist joke. If a woman senses that helping other women will hamper her career, she might be less likely to do so.

In the *Harvard Business Review,*[7] the authors of the study

---

6 D. R. Hekman et al., "Does diversity-valuing behavior result in diminished performance ratings for nonwhite and female leaders?" *Academy of Management Journal* (March 2016).

7 Stephanie K. Johnson and David R. Hekman, "Women and minorities are penalized for promoting diversity," *Harvard Business Review* (March 23, 2016).

point out that people tend to hire and promote people who look like them, which is one reason most top executives and leaders are still white men. If women are subtly punished for hiring people who look like them, then their numbers among the top echelon of the business world and in government will remain small.

When women do help each other, however, it has the same effect as when people help each other in general—we thrive. While thriving in matters of money is hardly the answer to everything, it *is* something we can actually measure. And business is definitely better as women take their places beside men in leadership roles.

In a landmark study of 7,280 leaders, researchers found that women were rated to be better leaders by their peers in fifteen out of sixteen characteristics.[8]

One explanation for why women make better leaders is that women who rise have done so because they are qualified and effective. Men tend to be more overconfident[9]—a tendency supported by various studies[10] and also by the fact that anyone who's reading this probably knows a few overconfident men, but not so many women who possess this less-than-endearing quality. That means that some men move up the ranks because they deserve it, while others advance because they're overconfident and

---

8 Jack Zenger and Joseph Folkman, "A study in leadership: Women do it better than men," *Harvard Business Review* (March 15, 2012).

9 A. Furnham et al., "Male hubris and female humility? A crosscultural study of ratings of self, parental, and sibling multiple intelligence in America, Britain, and Japan," *Intelligence* 30, no. 1 (2001).

10 V. Kuppuswamy and E. R. Mollick, "Hubris and humility: Gender differences in serial founding rates," https://ssrn.com/abstract=2623746 (June 26, 2015).

charismatic and have successfully promoted their inflated self-image.[11] In such cases, they are less effective as leaders.[12]

Here's another explanation of why women make better leaders: Julia Rozovsky, who evaluated work teams at Google to discover what made some of them more successful than others, concluded that people work better when they feel "psychologically safe."[13] Feeling safe in a work environment means having a manager who is sensitive and empathetic. Guys can definitely do that, but we do it more often.[14]

Women have everything to gain by working together and supporting one another. And on the off chance that Madeleine Albright was right, at the very least we should want to stay out of hell.

❖　❖　❖

Interesting Little Princess Fact #7

Traveling with a Little Princess can be hazardous to your suitcase. When Mari was four years old, we visited my sister's family

---

11 There's an elephant with a comb-over in the room, but I don't really want to talk about him in this book.

12 A. S. Shipman and M. D. Mumford, "When confidence is detrimental: Influence of overconfidence on leadership effectiveness," *Leadership Quarterly* 22, no. 4 (2011).

13 J. Rozovsky, "The five keys to a successful Google team," *The Water Cooler* (blog) (November 17, 2015).

14 L. Rueckert and N. Naybar, "Gender differences in empathy: The role of the right hemisphere," *Brain and Cognition* 67 (2008); M. V. Mestre et al., "Are women more empathetic than men? A longitudinal study in adolescence," *Spanish Journal of Psychology* 12, no. 1 (2009); and "Women are more empathetic toward their partner than men," Griffith University analysis of Household, Income and Labour Dynamics in Australia study (2014).

in New York and then my sister-in-law's family in England. Both families have an older girl who was formerly princess obsessed, and by the time we returned home, we'd inherited so many hand-me-down princess books that we had to buy an extra cheap suitcase to ensure we wouldn't have overweight baggage on our return flight home.

✦ ✦ ✦

Little Princess Pie

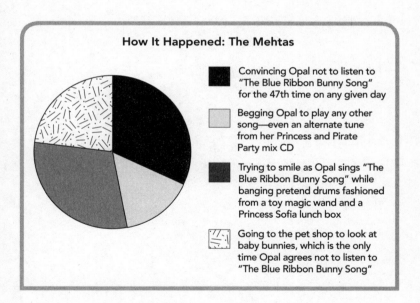

How It Happened: The Mehtas

Convincing Opal not to listen to "The Blue Ribbon Bunny Song" for the 47th time on any given day

Begging Opal to play any other song—even an alternate tune from her Princess and Pirate Party mix CD

Trying to smile as Opal sings "The Blue Ribbon Bunny Song" while banging pretend drums fashioned from a toy magic wand and a Princess Sofia lunch box

Going to the pet shop to look at baby bunnies, which is the only time Opal agrees not to listen to "The Blue Ribbon Bunny Song"

Opal Mehta has always loved music. Her mother, Anjali, is a classically trained pianist, so Opal had plenty of exposure to music in the womb and as a baby. One day, when she was two years old, her grandparents came over with a brand-new CD for Opal—it was an impulse buy at the Target checkout counter. Opal played it immediately and fell in love with one particular song—"The Blue Ribbon Bunny Song"—in which Clover the bunny raps to Princess Sofia about how awesome he is. It's the only song Opal listens to now. It's driving her mother bananas, which is why she has no remaining energy left to combat the princess effect.

Chapter 8

DO REAL PRINCESSES DO WINDOWS?

My Life in Pink:
THE HOUSEWORK MARTYR
RABBIT HOLE

Let's see if you've been paying attention. Time for a Little Princess Pop Quiz. Everyone pick up your pencils.

What Is the Bechdel Test?

If you haven't memorized chapter 1 yet, I'll save you the trouble of finding the correct passage. The Bechdel test determines whether or not a movie has at least two female characters in it who talk to each other about something other than a man. *Frozen* totally passed with frozen fractals all around.

Our Sleepy Trio of Cinderella, Snow White and Sleeping Beauty technically pass the test—the evil ladies of the house and Cinderella have conversations about going to a ball, for example—but in spirit these films fail. In spirit, these films are actually the poster children for Bechdel inadequacy, because the stories are all tales of women whose lives revolve around men.[1]

What's the problem with that exactly?

Feminists like me fear the Great Compromise, in which a woman gives up what's important to her in order to accommodate a man. When we then have Little Princesses who are dazzled by the Sleepy Trio, we worry that they'll be more inclined to follow that path. They might go from Little Princesses to boy-obsessed high schoolers to marriage-obsessed young adults to husband-obsessed wives.

Please excuse me as once again I have to go laugh uncontrollably for a moment. Talk amongst yourselves.

Okay, I'm back. Phew! Husband-obsessed wives! *(Wipes tears of laughter from cheek.)* That's a really good one.

I had friends who were man obsessed when I was young, free and single. But husband obsessed? I can't think of one wife I know who fits that description. We no longer enter into the institution of marriage to serve our husbands. Let's take a moment to thank the Second Wave of feminism for that. It's no small accomplishment, even though most of us take it for granted.

The mothers of middle-class Gen-Xers like me centered their lives around the orbit of Man. They did what their fathers told them and then went directly from the homes of their fathers to those of their husbands. As wives they cleaned, they cooked, they were the primary caretakers for their children—and this included

---

1 Charming, Ferdinand and Phillip are the princes' names. Sounds like a really bad law firm.

the women who worked outside the home. Their husbands might have helped them, but ultimately the burden of housework fell to the women. That was the only path they had. To be a woman of that generation who refused these roles you'd have to be . . . well, you'd have to be Betty Friedan.[2] You'd actually have to be a revolutionary.

My generation was different. Luckily for me—and thanks again to those Second Wave gals—no radical tendencies were necessary to become independent minded. By the time I went to college, women had the choice to opt out of traditional household roles. We could choose not to be married. We could choose romantic partners who were women—and we were the first generation allowed to do so openly. We could even choose to get married and share the household work equally with our husbands.

Yay, us!

And yet we failed! We had another path to take, and so many of us didn't take it.

Boo, us! How did this happen?

I offer the story of one such woman.

This is me. I call her Martyr Woman. That's not a pitchfork. It's supposed to be a broom.

---

2 Bonus fairy tale: Once upon a time there was a woman. Her name was Eve. She ate forbidden fruit and was punished with cramps and having a man rule over her and her XX-chromosomed offspring. That lasted about 6,000 years. Or maybe 200,000 years. Depends who you ask. Then, once upon another time, there was a fairy princess named Betty Friedan. She told women that they had done their time. Now they should be entitled not to have men rule over them anymore and to seek fulfilment outside the home. But she still couldn't do anything about the cramps.

For many years, I was a martyr. The cooking, the cleaning,[3] the primary parenting, the bill paying and the maintenance guy overseeing—this was all on me. Instead of eating Catalan tapas in Barcelona,[4] I was figuring out where the funky smell in the kitchen was coming from. I did everything in the house and I did it all with a glad and generous spirit.

I sense that you're rolling your eyes.[5] I guess the name Martyr Woman gave me away. Okay—I did it all with a begrudging and bitter spirit. I took care of the housework, but I resented it. I couldn't believe that the exact thing I had said would never happen to me—that I would be in charge of the thankless task of keeping house—happened. And with me as a willing participant.

This state unfortunately characterizes my generation. We were supposed to break free of traditional roles, yet we're still playing them.

The research on this topic is endless. The Working Mother Research Institute, the Bureau of Labor Statistics, the Pew

---

3 Though few people who enter my house suspect that any cleaning has been done to it.

4 That's just a random fantasy as opposed to what I was doing before marriage and children.

5 Valley Girl–style.

Research Center—any institution that studies this issue arrives at the same conclusion, which we all know anyway. Women usually do more housework, including in homes in which women work outside the house full-time.

Though the statistics highlight the problem, they don't explain how we stayed in these traditional roles. In my case, falling into the primary homemaker role was partially my fault. When Matt and I moved in together, I didn't cook more often than he did. We both did laundry and cleaned. I was sharing the load with my partner exactly as I'd imagined I would. I hadn't fallen down the "wife trap rabbit hole" and had created a new model for myself and any children we might have.

Then we actually had a child. This alone might not have changed everything, but the nail in the coffin of our household equality was that ten days after the child was born, he got sick.[6] Cai had a condition called pyloric stenosis, in which the pyloric muscle blocks the stomach so that no food can get in. Cai had a one in four chance of getting this condition, because Matt also had it as a baby. When Cai started projectile vomiting, we knew what was happening.

Pyloric stenosis is treated with surgery and Cai had an operation when he was two weeks old. During the five-day post-op phase, I wasn't allowed to nurse him. (Question: What happens to a baby who isn't allowed to nurse? Answer: He loses the ability to nurse.) We also had to constantly wake him to feed him sugar water with an eyedropper. (Question: What happens to a baby

6 This is how it happened in our marriage, but I bet everyone has a variation—a series of events that led them down the wife trap rabbit hole.

who is woken every hour? Answer: He loses his ability to *stay asleep.* For real. It happened.)

When Cai came home from the hospital, we joked that he looked like early, gaunt Sinatra. It was a sad sight indeed. My poor underweight newborn with haunted eyes was in dire need of love and care.

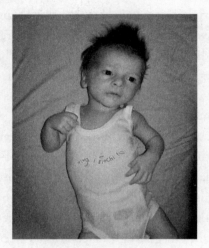

My underweight newborn.
(Photo credit: Worried Mother)

A few things happened after Cai's operation. I surrendered to having a weak, sleep-deprived newborn. It was liberating to give in to it—which I perhaps would not have been able to do without having taken the meditation/mindfulness course. After a few bumps (teaching him how to nurse and sleep again) it turned out to be a very peaceful time. I nursed Cai without wanting to be anywhere else. I cared for him without wanting to be anywhere else.

Meanwhile Matt fell into a depression. It's not uncommon for this to happen to men. A study in the *Journal of the American Medical Association* found that 10 percent of fathers of newborns suffered from depression, and in the period between three and six months after birth, the number rose to 25 percent.[7]

That's when it happened. As Matt withdrew, I fell down the wife trap rabbit hole. At first I didn't have a choice. I had to step in and take care of everything, because Matt was dropping out. Just like with depression, however, perhaps I didn't have to stay there for so long.

Looking back, I fell quickly and easily. I come from a home in which my mother did all the housework and most of the child care—so that was my model. And maybe I just liked being a martyr. That's not a joke. On some messed-up emotional level, I wanted to be one. I come from a long line of bitter women, each one of us a martyr. It's kind of my genetic destiny.

When Cai was a year and a half, Matt and I understood that our marriage was not working out the way either one of us wanted and we went into couples therapy. In one session Matt said, "I'd like to do more around the house." I distinctly remember not believing him. I sat there thinking, *Yeah, sure you do.* It was inconceivable that this person who had let me down genuinely wanted to do his share. I was certain this was just something he was saying because it sounded good and would absolve him from all the wrongs he had done.

I wasn't ready to let my martyrdom go. I mean—check out those boots. I was pretty attached.

Nor was I ready to give up control of the house. Though I'd been the kind of woman who said I wanted an equal marriage, at that moment here's what I actually wished: that I would continue

---

7 J. F. Paulson and S. D. Bazemore, "Prenatal and postpartum depression in fathers and its association with maternal depression: A meta-analysis," *Journal of the American Medical Association* 303, no. 19 (May 2010).

doing everything in the house and that Matt would appreciate, honor and love me for doing everything. I call this my 1950s fantasy. And true to that era, I resisted change.

Most of all, though, I clung to feeling like a victim, which is one of my depressive tendencies. I might have purged the victim identity from other aspects in my life, but in my primary relationship I was still addicted to suffering. Because as long as I could continue doing everything, I could maintain the conviction that I was completely right and he was completely wrong.[8]

He wasn't. Matt really did want to share the load. Depression had isolated him from the family and he wanted a way back in. It took me a while to figure that out. Therapy and being mindful helped—I observed how often my thoughts turned to anger and grievance. Slowly I let go of the tough bitch that had gotten my son through his newborn illness. I let go of my control of the house. And once again I let go of being a victim.

It took both of us working on the problem to address the gender inequality in our home. I'm lucky to have a husband who's genuinely interested in creating a new model. Matt's motivation was the same as mine. We wanted our marriage to work. We wanted our son to see past the stereotype of the traditional father who doesn't know how to locate the can opener in the kitchen.

Once we had a Little Princess, we had another motivation for breaking out of the stereotypically gender-specific patterns. We didn't want her to grow up to be Cinderella. She can mop the floors—floors get dirty, after all—but so can he, if there happens to be a "he" around. Though I'm happy to bequeath the boots to her, I'm hoping that the genetic line of martyred women ends

---

8 Oh, the pleasures of being right. They are deeply satisfying and hard to let go.

with me. Because the wife trap rabbit hole doesn't lead us to anywhere fun or surprising. It's just a muddy drag.

Princess Studies 101:
HOUSEWORK

Much like cleaning the toilet, let's just get this over with.

- In 2014, according to the Bureau of Labor Statistics, on an average day 49 percent of women did housework, such as cleaning or laundry, compared with 20 percent of men. And 69 percent of women were engaged with food preparation and cleanup, compared to 43 percent of men. Men were slightly more likely to engage in lawn and garden care than women—11 percent compared with 8 percent—and the numbers marked an improvement in the gender division of housework since 2003, when the bureau first started surveying what it calls "American Time Use."[9]

- In households where both partners work full-time, 41 percent of women reported doing more child care and 30 percent reported doing more chores, according to a "Women in the Workplace" survey by LeanIn.org and McKinsey & Company.[10]

- According to the Organisation for Economic Co-operation and Development (OECD), women spend more time on household chores than men in nearly every country surveyed,

---

9 Bureau of Labor Statistics, American Time Use Survey—2014 Results (2014).
10 McKinsey and Company, "Women in the Workplace" (September 2015).

with American women spending more than two hours a day on chores, compared to 82 minutes for men.[11]

I could go on, as every other day there seems to be a new study about women doing more housework than men, so if you don't believe me, just Google the subject and take your pick. I definitely believe me, because even though we've tried to do it otherwise, this imbalance resurfaces again and again in our house.

The "unpaid" work of women has different consequences depending on where and how you live. According to the UN special rapporteur on extreme poverty, this means that when unpaid work is taken into consideration, women in poorer countries work longer hours than men, but earn less money and receive less recognition. In these societies, women's unpaid work dominates their lives.

In countries like the United States, women doing more unpaid work has less dire consequences, though the imbalance still creates problems. It means women have less time to pursue a career, struggle more with a work-life balance and have less time, energy and resources than men.

In the previous chapter, I mentioned one reason why there are so few women in leadership roles—because women in positions of power don't always help other women on their way up. Another reason is the global phenomenon of women doing more unpaid labor than men.

The Gates Foundation addressed this issue in its 2016 annual letter, pointing out that in every society, women are expected to

---

11 Veerle Miranda, "Cooking, caring, and volunteering: Unpaid work around the world," *OECD Social, Employment, and Migration Working Papers*, no. 116 (September 2011).

do the unpaid work of cooking, cleaning and caring for the children and the elderly.

"Unless things change," Melinda Gates wrote, "girls today will spend hundreds of thousands more hours than boys doing unpaid work simply because society assumes it's their responsibility."[12]

If men shared the unpaid workload, which would allow for women's equal participation in the workforce, the economy would benefit.

In a 2015 report, the McKinsey Global Institute estimated that "if every country matched the gender parity of its fastest-improving neighboring region, global GDP could increase by $12 trillion in 2025."[13]

Just to put that in Little Princess terms, you'd have to make twelve thousand *Frozen*s to make that kind of money. I think even Mari would agree that is too many *Frozen*s.

Given the enormous potential benefit, why can't we crack this gender housework inequality nut?

Don't look at me. I'm sorry to report that even though we worked on it when Cai was a baby, I'm once again failing to share household responsibilities equally with my husband. As I started to write this book, Matt and I were still splitting the load. Matt was often the only father on the playground with the kids, one of the only fathers we knew who cooked regularly and was an equal partner in home maintenance. I felt great about it all, and proud of us, because we were creating a new model for our kids.

---

12 Melinda Gates, "Two superpowers we wish we had," Gates Notes Annual Letter (2016).

13 Jonathan Woetzel et al., "The Power of Parity: How advancing women's equality can add $12 trillion to global growth," *McKinsey Global Institute Report* (September 2015).

Then something changed. By the time I was finishing writing this book, some force had put a hex on our new model and then the clock struck midnight and we immediately turned into obsolescent husband and wife frogs. That force, of course, was money.

Matt took a job in an office. Before that we both worked from home, which made us very fortunate and also well suited to be equal partners. Matt took the job when the kids were eight and four. We moved our family from Jerusalem to Luxembourg, and it took about five minutes for my egalitarian ball gown to wither into threadbare rags. I took control of cooking, cleaning, laundry, apartment maintenance, grocery shopping and being the primary caretaker for our kids—feeding, clothing, homework, chauffeuring, medical appointments, after-school activities, teacher conferences, meltdown management, meltdown mismanagement, etc. . . .

As those who have done it know, it's not so simple to divide the housework when one partner works outside the home. Nor would it make sense for us. Matt was once a full-time writer, but he took the office job to support our family. He gave up something significant, so can I really complain about having become a housewife?

I couldn't unless I was a major bitch, and I'm only a little bitchy—mostly when I'm tired. This division is right for us at this stage of our lives. We're both contributing to our family and I'm not conflicted about what we have become. But neither can I pretend that I've created a new gender model for my kids. I haven't. Sorry, Cai and Mari. We did try.

Opposite of Serious

There seems to be a study every other day about how women still do more housework than men, so I decided to write one of my own.

Study on Household Inequality Sheds Light on Flying Fruit Epidemic

Women do anywhere between ten and twenty more hours of housework per week than their husbands do, according to a study released this week. Some women were surprised by the results.

"I'm floored," said Julie Marcus, a financial analyst. "On the other hand, this explains so much. Last night after dinner, my husband said, 'Thanks for that snack, honey,' and I threw a sack of navel oranges at him. I was, like, 'My goodness! Where is all this resentment coming from?' Now I understand!"

"I admit to being somewhat taken aback," a lab technician named Naomi Hyde said after reading an article about the findings. "I had no idea that laundry and cooking and grocery shopping and cleaning amounts to so many hours a week. But that definitely sheds light on my chronic fatigue, and also the fact that I hurled a cantaloupe at my husband while he was napping on the couch yesterday."

Some women acknowledged that they did more housework than their husbands, but said the disparity had not always been that way.

"When we first got married, we agreed to divide all the chores equally," Etta Glover, a human resources manager, explained. "And it worked! For about five minutes. Then we had a baby. Now I can't remember the last time a pomegranate made it through the day without being aimed at my husband's head."

Even though the study resonated with most women, a few defended the institution of marriage as totally worth it anyway.

"It's a trade-off," said Glover. "On the one hand, I do more housework. But on the other hand, I get to exhaustively research and plan our family vacation every year. So that's one whole week a year that I get to kick back and drink mojitos, while my husband plays in the swimming pool with the kids. Besides, what else would we do with the persimmons if I didn't propel them toward the love of my life?"

"What's the alternative?" said Hyde. "If I were unmarried, I might have much less housework to do, but I'd still get stuck changing the lightbulbs. And eating more bananas."

One woman pointed out that though the study was enlightening, it gave a false impression.

"It may be that I do most of the housework," said attorney Greta Miller, "but that doesn't tell the whole story. I'm also the primary caregiver for our toddler, and responsible for everything that goes along with child care for the older ones. I do the homework with the kids, for example. And the baths. Packing their lunches and schoolbags. Birthday party planning. School plays. Teacher meetings. Staying home on their sick days. Medical stuff. Driving them absolutely everywhere. What was my point again? Oh, yeah. That my husband reads them a story each and every night just after I slingshot a Bosc pear his way. It's the absolute sweetest!"

When asked if they would like the balance in their homes to change, the women gave varied answers.

"It depends what you mean by that question," said Glover. "If the question is, 'Do you wish that your husband would share the work more equally?' then the answer is, 'Sure. Why not?' But if the question is, 'Do you wish that your husband would somehow magically transform himself into a berry-eating Centaur?' then my answer would be exactly the same."

"Frankly, I can't imagine it any other way," Marcus said. "I mean, I'm thinking about what it would be like if my husband was the one doing the extra housework. And it would be, like, you know. It would be . . . Actually, sorry, I *can* imagine it. Does anyone have a stalk of rhubarb handy?"

Some women expressed the hope that younger, Millennial women would share the housework more equally with their partners.

"That's exactly what our mothers thought it would be like for us—more equality between us and our husbands," Miller said. "So, yeah. Maybe their hope skipped our generation and will go to the next one? Only time will tell. But there's a watermelon sale over at the Stop & Shop, so I gotta run."

"I'm not really bothered about the findings," said Hyde. "I mean, look at Hillary Clinton. She probably did those extra hours of housework for years. And even though some believe she had the more promising career when they graduated Yale Law School, her husband got to be president first. It's okay, though, because now she'll finally have her turn! Or not.[14] Whatever."

Opposite of Serious

Once I fell back into housewife mode, I noticed patterns emerging that were familiar from my childhood. When my kids misplaced something, they immediately asked me if I knew where it was— Matt was spared ever finding the microscopic sword that went with the Playmobil knight, for example. He had no idea what I packed the kids for lunch and would occasionally ask me vexing questions like, "Where do we keep the toilet paper again?" and

---

14 This was written before November 2016.

"How do you turn the oven on?" and "What time do the kids start school?" One time I was planning to spend the day away from home—the plans were canceled and it never happened—and I was appalled by how meticulously I'd need to plan the whole thing, especially because when Matt goes away on business, zero planning is needed.

This home-related cluelessness isn't good for either of us and, like everything else, we're working on it. But because humor is my therapy I wrote this satirical piece.

Notes for My Husband During My Overnight Trip

Hi, honey. By the time you read this, I'll probably already be in the air. Good morning! I hope the kids didn't wake you up too early. Ha-ha-ha. Of course they did!

Here's the list of what you need to do this morning.

1. Defrost five slices of whole wheat bread. The package is in the freezer in a bag marked "Whole Wheat Bread."

2. Sorla's and Kamen's clothing is laid out for them at the foot of their beds. They can dress themselves. Zippy likes to choose her own clothing, which is why the bottom shelf is a heap of Hello Kitty T-shirts and tutus. Just let her try on as many outfits as she wants.

3. If Zippy has slept past 5:30, she should get a sticker for her "sleepy time" chart, which is hanging on the refrigerator. Make sure to give her one of either the dinosaur stickers or the sparkly heart stickers, which are on top of the microwave. Do *not* give her the googly eye stickers because she will pop them in her mouth and laugh that she's "eating eyeballs." Actually, never mind. I'll just go ahead and hide them now.

4. Toast two pieces of toast lightly, spread a little honey on them and give them to Sorla with a half-filled cup of milk. Toast two more pieces even more lightly than that, butter them, make a sandwich, remove the crusts, cut into fours and give them to Kamen with a cup of apple juice. When Kamen comes to the table with his ninja sword, tell him he must keep it on his lap at *all times* or he will not get goldfish crackers for lunch. Spread the "nut" spread on a fifth piece and put it on the princess plate for Zippy. She will not eat it, but if it's not there, she's likely to go ballistic. Hand Zippy her sippy cup of water.

5. The lunches are packed and already in the backpacks along with water bottles, completed homework and signed permission slips for the school trips. Please do not let Zippy near any of the backpacks because she will drop the contents into the cage with Fluffy.

6. If Sorla starts crying and saying she hates school, promise her an extra ten minutes on the iPad tonight. Please keep Zippy away from Sorla.

7. By now, Zippy will have unscrewed her sippy cup, spilled it on her shirt and undressed completely. This is your opportunity to take her for a pee. Afterward, let her return to her shelf to try on new outfits. When she starts to whine that she has "nothing to wear," give her the polka-dotted dress that's on my dresser and promise her a pink marshmallow if she "puts it on nicely." If she puts it on backward, *do not* adjust it or you will have to start all over again.

8. Kamen will be trying to fit his sword into his backpack. He will figure out on his own that it doesn't fit, so just let him have a go. If Sorla is still miserable, throw a few goldfish crackers at her and promise her an additional ten minutes on the iPad.

9. Time for shoes and socks. Good luck with that!

10. Tear Zippy's breakfast into little pieces and put it in a ziplock bag. Seal the bag. Do not give it to her until you are outside the door; otherwise, she will pour the contents into Fluffy's cage.

11. Zippy will be the first to be ready to go. Then she'll get bored. She'll either grab Kamen's sword and run into our bedroom or she'll start throwing things at Sorla. Whatever she does, it's imperative that you *do not raise your voice*. Trust me on this one. I know it's bad right around now, but once you raise your voice, Zippy will be inconsolable.

12. If you have raised your voice, Zippy will be having her morning tantrum. Grab the bag of pink marshmallows on the counter. No—those are the fish crackers. It's the other bag. The pink one. That's it. Now step outside the door and say, "Whoever gets outside first gets a marshmallow!" Once everyone is on the other side of the threshold, give one to Zippy no matter who reaches you first. While Zippy is doing her marshmallow dance, secretly slip marshmallows to Kamen and Sorla.

13. I'm probably so drunk right now! I've made separate afternoon and evening lists for you. See you tomorrow. Love you!

❖ ❖ ❖

Interesting Little Princess Fact #8

In Mari's preschool, all the kids designed their own robot and were asked questions about it, like, "What is your robot called?" and "Where does your robot live?" and "What sorts of things does it do?" Mari's answers: The robot is called "Beauty." It lives in a castle. It makes princesses out of blocks and also turns princes into princesses.

✦ ✦ ✦

Little Princess Pie

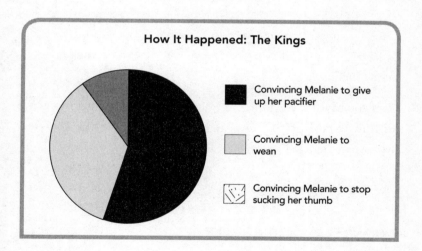

When Amy King was a teenager, she hated having braces with a passion. She promised herself that when she became a parent, she'd never force her children to have perfect teeth. But a few years after she gave birth to Melanie, Amy realized that letting an adolescent girl have crooked teeth wasn't a realistic solution, either. After Amy read an article about how pacifiers and thumb sucking and late weaning might possibly increase the chance that a child will need braces, she began to do everything in her power to coax Melanie away from her desperate need to suck stuff.

That's why Melanie is now allowed to sleep, eat and watch videos inside a pop-up princess castle play tent.

Chapter 9

FEMINIST FAIRY TALES

My Life in Pink:
THERE'S SOMETHING AWESOME IN THE STATE OF YOU-KNOW-WHERE

When Mari was about five months old we went to a friend's house for a Hanukkah party. Isn't socializing with babies fun? I spent most of the time following Mari around to make sure she didn't swallow a Lego piece or pull the tablecloth and send platters of poached salmon tumbling through the festive air.

While Mari was briefly stationary, I chatted with a woman for a few minutes. She was a successful journalist with two older kids. In midconversation I cut our chat short, because Mari was crawling toward a staircase that led downstairs.

"Sorry about that," I said, springing into action.

"Don't worry," the woman called after me. "They get older. You get your dignity back!"

As my baby was headed toward a stairwell, I didn't have time to respond to her helpful prediction. But later on, I wondered about the assumptions behind her words. If they reflect how she sees the world, then she believes:

- That chasing a baby around a party means you have no dignity.

- That I must have been unhappy because I had a baby and was robbed of the opportunity to socialize.[1]

- That having older kids who needed me less often would make me happier.

It was funny, because I had never felt happier than when my kids were babies. The reason, I know, was a combination of my oxytocin high[2] and the fact that I was able to surrender to the moment so often. There were certainly times when I didn't want to be with my babies. Mostly, though, I just wanted to be with them.

The dignity comment reflects a problem that our Little Princesses have, and it's a problem that extends beyond what we do or don't do in our own homes. Because even if the princess culture doesn't inflict lasting damage to their self-esteem, and even if Cinderella's story doesn't persuade them that all they need to do is look pretty to be happy, we still live in a society that devalues the feminine.

---

1 This one is especially funny for introverts, for whom making small talk with people you don't know is about as fun as making tissue paper pom-poms for a bridal shower.

2 After my kids were born, I experienced an amazing high caused by oxytocin, a hormone that's released when you give birth and breastfeed. Other oxytocin boosters: dancing, spending time and bonding with people you love, being kind, meditating, exercising, cuddling with people and animals and having sex. Go get yourself some oxytocin today!

This deprecation manifests itself in various ways. One is that the United States is the only wealthy country not to offer family-friendly policies like paid maternity leave. As maternity leave is a policy that helps working women, the failure of the United States to provide leave is evidence that the country does not support, encourage or value working women.

More than 120 countries have paid maternity leave—including nations with much lower GDP rankings than the United States, such as Bulgaria, Chile and Greece. Sweden has fifty-six weeks. Canada has fifty.[3] American women, however, generally have the choice to "opt out"—choose parenting over career—or return to work, which means choosing career over being with their baby. I use the word "choose," but many women don't have that choice. Most women either can't afford to work, because child care is too expensive, or they can't afford *not* to return to work, in which case there are no good solutions.

Some countries also have paid paternity leave. In fact, Sweden reserves some of the family leave for dads. Remember our sad statistics about housework inequality? Once it's established that the woman is the one to stay home with the baby, it follows that this stay-at-home parent will be the one to do most of the house-work and also fall into the role of primary caretaker of the child. That means when mothers go back to work, they're often still the primary caretaker, because that's the system everyone got used to.

In countries where paternity leave is offered, the men who take it exercise their parenting muscles. Their brains even change

---

3 The lack of family leave has a negative impact on child development, children's health, the mental health of parents and the overall well-being of families, according to the president of the American Academy of Pediatrics, Dr. Benard Dreyer. ("A pediatrician's view of paid parental leave," interview, NPR, *All Things Considered*, October 10, 2016.)

to become more "maternal." A study conducted by the Gonda Brain Sciences Center of Bar-Ilan University found that fathers who were primary caregivers underwent brain activity similar to that which is usually experienced by mothers.[4] A separate study found that fathers who interact with their babies secrete oxytocin, the happy hormone that made me feel like all was right with the world when I held my babies.[5]

There are multiple benefits to men bonding with their babies. Fathers who take paternity leave end up spending more time caring for children later on and more time participating in housework. But the brain study also sheds light on the idea that most of us don't have a brain that is fully male or female. If our brains are a mosaic of both male and female qualities, and if life experiences influence how the brain connects and functions, then it makes sense that men who have the opportunity to explore their feminine side—by being fathers to newborns, for example— might feel more complete. My husband is one of them. I can't assume all men are like him, but some are, and I'd wager that most men would be better off if they were allowed to explore and develop their nurturing, sensitive side.

The point is that the more we give both men and women the opportunity to explore both "gender" sides, the better off we'll be individually. The more room we give women to be in the workplace with equal opportunity for pay and advancement, and the more room we give men to be at home with the family, the better off we'll all be.

---

4 E. Abraham et al., "Father's brain is sensitive to childcare experiences," *Proceedings of the National Academy of Sciences* 111 no. 27 (2014).

5 Ilanit Gordon et al., "Oxytocin and the development of parenting in humans," *Biological Psychiatry* 68, no. 4 (August 15, 2010).

It sounds like a fairy tale, yet why should it be? Every individual is different. Some might thrive more at home or at work, but most of us would benefit from finding an individualized work-life balance. The happiest countries in the "Happiest Countries" surveys are always the ones with the best work-life balance. Take the happiest place on earth. Can you guess what it is?

That's right! It's Denmark! My sixth grade country, Denmark, is the happiest place on earth! Some people say Disney's Magic Kingdom is the "Happiest Place on Earth," but according to the UN World Happiness Report and other studies like it, it's the home country of Walt Disney's favorite fairy-tale writer, Hans Christian Andersen.[6] In light of this data, I'm going to write a sequel to my school report right this very moment.

Denmark: A Country

What is Denmark?

Denmark is a country in northern Europe that is part of Scandinavia. Copenhagen is the capital of Denmark.

Denmark is a country where the people have liberal joint parental leave laws and a high female employment rate, and fathers who participate in child care more than fathers in other countries.[7] Denmark has affordable, tax-subsidized child care, which enables parents

---

6 Hans Christian Andersen wrote *The Snow Queen*, in case you haven't been paying attention. Walt Disney wanted to adapt *The Snow Queen* for film but the project stalled for many years. After he died, the story was finally adapted and became *Frozen*.

7 P. Gracia and G. Esping-Andersen, "Fathers' child care time and mothers' paid work: A cross-national study of Denmark, Spain, and the United Kingdom," *Family Science* 6, no. 1 (2015).

to return to work. Danes are also the reason Frozen *is a movie. Danes are much, much better than you.*

✦ ✦ ✦

I'm kidding! Danes aren't better than you, but their government does have policies that make better sense for its people.

Policies like family leave help everyone. Remember the McKinsey study about how the world could increase its global GDP by twelve thousand *Frozens*? In the United States, according to that study, up to $4.3 trillion could be added to the annual GDP in 2025 if women attain full gender equality. Family leave—including paternity leave—is the cornerstone of that particular dream.

Which brings me back to the idea that having babies robs you of dignity. That's the assumption of someone living in a country that values work above family. I'm not knocking the woman who said it to me—her attitude reflects accepted ideas. Hers is a common assumption among Americans. When we're raised to worship work and money, we devalue family. When we devalue family, the primary parenting falls to the women, because women are also devalued. When we value family and parenting, men are more likely to share in it and that benefits everybody. (And if a man was chasing a baby who was heading toward a stairwell, I'm fairly certain that no one would tell him that his "lost dignity" may yet be restored with the passage of time.)

Denmark doesn't just have a high female employment rate—it has one of the highest employment rates in general. It has the kind of strong economy some American politicians promise to procure for voters, while at the same time they criticize welfare. Welfare benefits like family leave don't drain the economy, however. They are the backbone of a healthy work culture, which includes both genders and doesn't maximize the potential of one at the expense of the other.

Expanding the reach of the feminine has no downside. Neither does recognizing that gender is a spectrum and not two distinct definitions of two genders that must always be opposite. The idea of a mosaic brain rather than the binaries of "male" and "female" brains can free us from so many damaging expectations and limitations.

But let's get real. We don't live in this egalitarian fairy tale. We're not there yet. Men are still men. Women still know where the can openers are, because that's what's expected of them.

All this raises a question for me as the mother of a Little Princess. What Mari wants now—pink and princesses—is accepted and encouraged by society, but what she wants will change. If her needs and goals are at odds with the world in which I'm raising her, which is often the case for adolescent girls and women, she's going to have a problem.

I loved the scene in *Frozen* where Elsa expresses herself for the first time since childhood, letting the magic flow from her fingers and creating a breathtaking palace carved from ice. To get to that place of authenticity, she first had to isolate herself.

Sometimes I wonder if by encouraging my daughter to be herself, I'm setting her up to feel isolated. If I manage to raise a daughter who stays true to herself, will she be more likely to live in conflict with society? Am I dooming her, in a sense, to be alone?

To be continued . . .

Opposite of Serious

A study published by the Harvard Business School asserted that working mothers have more successful daughters. All I could think about as I read the study was the stay-at-home mothers who had just cleaned vomit from car seats, reading this study and shaking their heads with that magical combination of exasperation, exhaustion and guilt. That image inspired this satirical piece.

Working Mothers Have More Successful Daughters, According to Recent Depressing Study

Working mothers have more successful daughters and more caring sons, according to a recent study conducted by researchers at the Harvard Business School. The study suggests that the daughters of working mothers are more likely to work, to be in a supervisory position and to earn more money than daughters of women who don't work outside the home.

"After reading the study, I feel even more useless than usual," said stay-at-home mom Melissa Gretz, who came across the study in her Facebook feed while her two-year-old twins were napping in the next room. "Because it means that not only am I failing to have a meaningful career, but my daughters, to whom I have dedicated so much time and attention, are also doomed to be unproductive and unfulfilled."

But it's not only the daughters of stay-at-home mothers who underperform compared to the daughters of mothers who work. Sons of gainfully employed mothers spend more time caring for family members than sons of stay-at-home mothers do, according to the same study.

"That was particularly hurtful to read," said SAHM Laura Shafer. "Because I did go back to work after taking unpaid maternity leave. Then I had a second baby and realized there was no way I could return to my sixty-hour workweek. And now as a result, my son will be a deadbeat twit."

The Harvard study follows another recent survey that was widely reported and shared on social media. That study indicates that working mothers are also more likely to have satisfying romantic relationships with partners who respect them for contributing to society. Husbands of mothers who don't work, in contrast, spend a significant portion of their day either resenting their unemployed wives or wondering what they do all day.

Husbands of working mothers are also more likely to find their wives sexually attractive.

"It completely rings true for me," said Mark Jarvis, whose wife, Frieda, decided to stay at home with their children because of the prohibitive cost of child care. "I mean, every time Frieda tells me about what a rough day she's had with the kids, it's like a missile directed at my libido."

"After I had our first baby, we added up the numbers and realized that my work as a palliative care nurse wouldn't really be enough to justify sending our child to day care," Frieda added. "But when we made that decision, I never imagined it would lead to the end of my romantic connection to my husband. Isn't life funny?"

Men married to women who stay at home with their children are twice as likely to have extramarital affairs, according to the survey.

"Ha-ha-ha—that's just crazy talk!" said Mark.

Working mothers are also generally thinner than stay-at-home mothers, have more lustrous hair and are usually better dressed than their full-time-mom counterparts, according to the soul-crushing findings.

"That doesn't surprise me at all," said Gretz, "because sometimes I feel like yoga pants are my best friend." Gretz says she was slightly taken aback, however, by yet another research paper that she read when a former colleague helpfully e-mailed her the link with the words STOP WHATEVER YOU'RE DOING AND READ THIS in the subject line. According to the findings, stay-at-home mothers are more likely to abuse alcohol than working mothers, are more prone to become addicted to prescription drugs and are ninety-nine times more likely to keep their destructive vices a secret so that they can feel even more isolated and guilt-ridden.

"The United States is the only developed country that does not guarantee paid maternity leave," said a male politician. "So we shouldn't be too alarmed by any of these studies, because Uncle Sam knows what he's doing."

Opposite of Serious

20 Ways to Erode a First-Time Mom's Self-Esteem

1. Ask her if she's lost her baby weight.

2. When she says she's not getting much sleep, tell her, "I could tell by looking at you."

3. Ask her how much sleep the baby is getting, and regardless of what she tells you, scowl.

4. Tell her how crucial it is for brain development to get the baby to sleep through the night.

5. Tell her how crucial it is for brain development not to let the baby cry too much.

6. Say, "Is he/she a good baby?"

7. Ask her if she's doing her Kegels.

8. Ask her what she does all day.

9. When she says she's surprised that she has no time to sit down and eat a meal, tell her to look at it as an opportunity to start losing that baby weight.

10. Ask her if she's unstimulated and worried that her brain is going soft.

11. Offer some helpful statistics about the failure of mothers to return to the workforce.

12. Offer some more helpful statistics about the failure of couples to resume a healthy sex life after having a baby.

13. Point out that she has dried spit-up on her shirt.

14. Inhale deeply and say, "Wow, I sure have missed that spit-up smell!"

15. Ask her if she's lonely and feeling friendless.

16. Ask her if she's worried about developing postpartum depression.

17. Remind her how lucky she is and ask her if she feels lucky every second of every waking hour.

18. Say, "Do you feel like your life is over now?"

19. Ask her if she can fit into all her pre-pregnancy clothing yet.

20. Ask her when she's going back to work. When she answers, scowl.

✦ ✦ ✦

Interesting Little Princess Fact #9

Every time the parent of a princess-obsessed little boy loves, encourages and accepts his or her child just as he is, a fairy gets her wings. Every time a playground parent says, "You shouldn't let him play with girl toys or dress up like a princess," a fairy sticks her finger down her throat and pretends to hurl. And then dies.

✦ ✦ ✦

Little Princess Pie

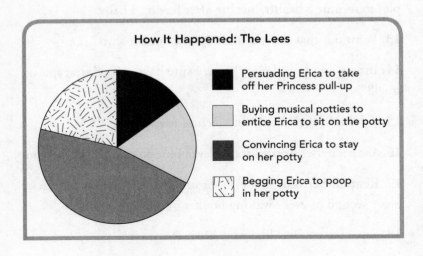

How It Happened: The Lees

- Persuading Erica to take off her Princess pull-up
- Buying musical potties to entice Erica to sit on the potty
- Convincing Erica to stay on her potty
- Begging Erica to poop in her potty

Erica Lee pooped on her potty once, and the family rejoiced. But since that hallowed day, Erica has refused to poop on her potty or in the toilet. She'll sit on the potty for forty-five minutes, and then because it's way past her bedtime, her mother, Felicia, will give up and put princess Pull-Ups on her. Erica poops thirty seconds later.

Ordinarily, Felicia would never push Erica into something she isn't ready to do, but she is eight months pregnant, and the idea of having two children who don't poop in the toilet makes her head spin. Felicia has no energy left to combat the princess effect. She recently promised Erica she'd purchase an $80 Disney Princess Royal 2-Sided Kitchen & Café if Erica starts pooping on her potty.

Chapter 10

PRINCESS PERFECT

My Life in Pink:
THE WOLF IN THE WOODS

Readers might recall that my husband, Matt, and I were both a bit of a fixer-upper. Relationship-wise, we were like a couple of Floridians unexpectedly parachuted into Oymyakon, Russia, in November—ill equipped to be there and with no idea of what we were doing. We were bad at communicating, unpracticed at connecting and generally a mess.

What made us such dunces? I'd refer you to our couples therapist, who can give you all the scintillating details,[1] but since she's sworn to professional secrecy I'll break it down: Fear lay at the root of my intimacy problems—fear of making myself vulnerable, of getting hurt and of being rejected. Matt's ineptitude stemmed

---

1 It's not for nothing that we pay them. If the details were interesting, someone else would listen to our problems.

from a malady that he happens to share with princesses. He needed to be perfect.

Perfectionism is an unsurprising relationship buster. Perfectionists rarely say they're sorry, since apologies are for people with flaws. They're highly critical of themselves and their loved ones. They have no room to be human or show vulnerabilities, and they're sometimes devastated when the perfect image they have of themselves doesn't match the imperfect reality.

Time for a Little Princess Pop Quiz. You already know what to do with your pencils.

1. *Why did Elsa run?*

ANSWER: Elsa ran because she was afraid to hurt the people she loved and because she was tired of hiding her true self.

2. *Why did Elsa sing?*

ANSWER: Elsa sang because she finally expressed her true self. But she was only able to do this away from society. If it had been up to Elsa, she would have remained alone.

"Yes, I'm alone, but I'm alone and free." That's one of my favorite lyrics from that song. What are yours?

In the previous chapter I asked if raising my daughter to be herself would doom her to be alone. If I manage to raise an authentic son, I can more easily imagine he'd be accepted. Or at least, I believe he'd be accepted more than rejected. Men who are in touch with their emotions and needs can find their people, unless they're still living in cultures in which "tough guy" is still the grooviest compliment for dudes.

It's trickier for girls and women. We're bombarded with critique anytime we show our true selves. Women who express themselves online are routinely harassed and threatened, which are techniques used to subdue and silence women. From a young age, girls are encouraged to be inauthentic because when they speak their mind, they're called aggressive. When they express emotion, they're dismissed as weak and annoying. When they speak up in the Senate, they're told to shut up.[2]

Girls and women are expected to be docile, perfect beings. In chapter 6, I talked about the expectations to be docile and silent, traits that characterize the early Disney princesses. The pressure to be perfect, however, extends beyond the reach of the Sleepy Trio.

The expectation to be perfect is what underlies the beauty industry, the advertising industry, the enormous volume of books and articles dedicated to achieving professional and parenting success, and Internet culture in general.

---

2 This is a reference to what happened to Senator Elizabeth Warren on February 7, 2017. She was formally silenced by her male colleagues when she tried to read a letter by Coretta Scott King in opposition to Jeff Sessions's confirmation as attorney general. The following day, male senators were allowed to read the same letter uninterrupted on the Senate floor.

Many have written and spoken eloquently about this damaging pressure to be perfect and "have it all" and how to address it.[3] As the mother of a Little Princess, what concerns me is how that need to be perfect erases the space in which we can be real. Because that is at the heart of the princess problem. The Sleepy Trio aren't real characters—they are projected images of perfection. They aren't just ordinary perfect cream puffs, either. Snow White, Cinderella and Sleeping Beauty are paradigms of cream-puffery, created by and for men, formed for the sole purpose of looking pretty and marrying for their salvation.

So how do we raise Little Princesses who absorb a different message from the one that almost sabotaged my marriage? What's the best way to teach kids that they don't need to be perfect?

Before we answer this one, let's first name the real wolf lurking in the woods. It's not princesses. It's not even perfectionism. It's shame.

Brené Brown is a research professor whose TED Talk on the subject of shame, "The Power of Vulnerability," has been viewed 29 million times. According to Brown, social scientists believe that the ability to feel connected to other people is what gives meaning and purpose to our lives. Shame, says Brown, is the fear of disconnection. Shame is the fear that there is something about us—maybe we're not pretty enough or rich enough or smart enough or "fill-in-your-own-blank" enough—which, if discovered, makes us unworthy of connection.

The way to connect with other people, according to Brown, is "to allow ourselves to be seen, really seen." And the people who

---

3 Like Anne-Marie Slaughter, Debora Spar and Jean Kilbourne, among others.

do this, she says, embrace vulnerability and have the courage to be imperfect.

That spoke to me—and presumably to some 29 million other people. The reason I'm still married is because Matt and I both learned how to do this. We learned how to accept our own vulnerabilities, how to allow them to be seen by each other and how to accept the weaknesses in each other. We learned how to get hurt and to forgive—which are both connected to accepting imperfection. Forgiving someone who has hurt you and making yourself vulnerable all over again is part of staying in a marriage, or at least, it's part of staying in a marriage not dominated by resentment and grievance and cold shoulders.

It's hard. Anyone who has been in a long-term relationship understands how complex this is. Neither Matt nor I is wired to do this, but we know we have no choice if we want to stay together. If fear and the desire to be perfect were the impulses that almost doomed our relationship, accepting flaws and vulnerability is what transformed our marriage into something satisfying and lasting. This is our marital silver bullet. It's the reason we can connect. It's why we love each other, rather than the idea of each other.

It's also my blueprint for how to be a parent to my Little Princess.

When their baby stages ended, I fell out of love with my kids. After I stopped breastfeeding, my oxytocin levels plummeted and my constant high was lost. All I was left with was two helpless little people with runny noses, poor impulse control and whiny voices.

Shockingly, my kids behave like children. They are sometimes amazing and loving beyond anything I could have imagined, and other times they're demanding, combative, defiant, hurtful, illogical and utterly bananas. They do upsetting things without meaning to, but they also behave in ways to deliberately test me and my patience and my love. Occasionally they're hungry, and their hunger causes them to act like exasperating brats, and yet they *still refuse to eat*. Other times they're tired, and their exhaustion causes them to act like frightening loons, and yet they *still refuse to sleep*. They have this thing where they fight with each other *all the f#?@ing time* about *the stupidest f#?@ing s#$t*. Sometimes at the end of the day all I want to do is bury my head in a bottle of wine, which is why "Mommy Drinking" is a thing we all know and love and hate. This feeling arose more than ever when Matt started a full-time job. At the same time, the kids started at a new school and their school day ended at 12:45. You do the math.

On bad days, I fall into a trap. I think, "All I need to be happy is to go away."

These are certainly champagne problems—in fact, these are perhaps the most champagniest problems of them all, aside from algae in your swimming pool and not getting a reservation at the new gastronomic boutique bistro that serves white truffle shavings and caviar on top of your saffron-infused lobster—but they are my problems nonetheless. The bottom line is that as my children grow up, I don't want my love to dry up into a tight wad of exhausted, frustrated resentment.

And the cure to not wanting to be with my children, funnily enough, is to be with my children. Because when I experience those thoughts of running away and isolating myself from the people I love the most, I'm shutting down. I'm going to that place where I'm cut off from love and compassion and where I could easily slip into sadness and depression.

But if during those moments I let myself be with them—really be with them without judgment and expectation—then I open up to them again. That's not just the paradox of parenting. It's pretty much the paradox of every relationship. The key is the one I learned when I left depression behind and the same one that saved my marriage. It's to welcome imperfection and vulnerability. It's to accept, accept, accept.

When my children behave badly, in the exact way that invites me to reject them, it's an opportunity for me to accept them completely, flaws and all. I don't nail this every time, but I'm trying. I'm trying for myself and for my kids and also because the most powerful way to combat the princess effect is to let the people in our lives know that they don't need to be perfect to be unconditionally loved.

I didn't come up with this concept, by the way. It's called parenting and many of us had parents who gave us unconditional love—and I'm very sorry to those who didn't have this—and emotionally limited people like me only really learn how to do this after we become parents. Matt and I, for example, only got there after we had a baby. Obviously you can figure out this life hack without having kids, but my school of unconditional love and acceptance of humans—with all their wonderful gifts and weaknesses and joys and neuroses and creativity and stubbornness and generosity and unpredictability and vulnerabilities and pink proclivities—was the school of motherhood.

It's a really terrific school. I highly recommend it.

There's another benefit to raising children who accept weakness and vulnerability, and who have compassion for imperfection. We live on a planet where some people are lucky, and others are not. When children are raised to dismiss, ignore and judge the weak and the vulnerable members of our society, then we have certainly failed as parents. As we raise our Little Princesses and all our children, it's crucial to cultivate and teach acceptance and compassion. We may not live in a perfect fairy tale, but we can certainly make the world better than it is now.

Princess Studies 101:
PERFECTIONISM

Disney's Sleepy Trio was perfect. Is that so wrong?

Clinical psychologists Paul Hewitt and Gordon Flett have researched the effects of perfectionism for more than twenty years. They created a multidimensional scale that distinguishes between three types of perfectionism: "Self-oriented" perfectionists have high personal standards; "other-oriented" perfectionists direct their standards outward, which means they demand perfection from others; and "socially prescribed" perfectionists perceive that others demand perfection from them, whether it's a spouse, friend, colleague or society in general.

While some believe being a perfectionist can be functional—and even a good thing—many psychologists disagree. Hewitt and Flett have found that perfectionism correlates with depression,[4] anxiety,[5] negative body image and eating disorders[6] and other

4 P. L. Hewitt and G. L. Flett, "Dimensions of perfectionism in unipolar depression," *Journal of Abnormal Psychology* 100, no. 1 (1991).

5 G. L. Flett et al., "Self-oriented perfectionism, neuroticism and anxiety," *Personality and Individual Differences* 10, no. 7 (1989).

6 P. L. Hewitt et al., "Perfectionism traits and perfectionistic self-presentation in eating disorder attitudes, characteristics, and symptoms," *International Journal of Eating Disorders* 18, no. 4 (1995).

mental health problems.[7] Aside from the mental health issues, people who are perfectionists tend to procrastinate,[8] have relationship problems and experience burnout, "a syndrome associated with chronic stress that manifests as extreme fatigue, perceived reduced accomplishment and eventual detachment."[9]

A 2014 paper published in the *Review of General Psychology* found "consistent evidence linking suicide ideation with chronic exposure to external pressures to be perfect."[10] Other research has also found that boys who committed suicide felt pressure to hide their true selves "behind a mask."[11]

Where do the princesses fit into all of this?

Like all images of perfection absorbed by children, the risk is that they'll believe that being "princess perfect" is a worthy goal. It's not, of course. Just the idea of being perfect is a recipe for unhappiness and other more serious problems. This is a book about Little Princesses, but boys are susceptible to this mind trap as well. So are adults. We replace princesses with celebrities and successful people. Our exposure to the cult of celebrity and perfection has increased exponentially with Internet culture, as has our tendency to promote and project the idea that everything in

---

7 P. L. Hewitt and G. L. Flett, "Perfectionism in the self and social contexts: Conceptualization, assessment, and association with psychopathology," *Journal of Personality and Social Psychology* 60, no. 3 (1991).

8 G. L. Flett et al., "Components of perfectionism and procrastination in college students," *Social Behavior and Personality* 20, no. 2 (1992).

9 A. P. Hill and T. Curran, "Multidimensional perfectionism and burnout: A meta-analysis," *Personality and Social Psychology Review* 20, no. 3 (2016).

10 G. L. Flett et al., "The destructiveness of perfectionism revisited: Implications for the assessment of suicide risk and the prevention of suicide," *Review of General Psychology* 18, no. 3 (2014).

11 A. W. Törnblom et al., "Shame behind the masks: The parents' perspective on their sons' suicide," *Archives of Suicide Research* 17, no. 3 (2013).

our lives is perfect. That's the recurring theme of what people share on Facebook and Instagram and other social media platforms I don't know about yet because I'm too old.

So how do we help our Little Princesses navigate a society that idealizes perfection? A phenomenally successful princess movie contains some wisdom on this subject, and it's pretty awesome. The heroine, by the way, isn't the most popular Disney princess of all time. It's her sister.

Hang on to your sleds, folks. We're almost there.

Opposite of Serious

Remember the book French Women Don't Get Fat? *The concept of the book was to teach American women how to "not get fat," yet also enjoy pastry and wine and three-course meals by living as French women do. Some of the advice in the book is sensible—such as walking more and eating less and enjoying life—however, the notion that French women have all the answers is laughable. At the time the book was published, France was one of the worst countries in Western Europe for women, according to the World Economic Forum's* Global Gender Gap Report. *Its ranking has since improved and, yes, that's at least in part due to progressive gender-equality legislation.*

I'm sure that American and French societies could learn something from each other, but the idea that women from other countries are always better than American women became the theme of a whole genre of books. The popularity of these books doesn't tell me that American women are inferior—it just shows how often women are encouraged to feel dissatisfied and self-critical. I made fun of the trend in this satirical piece.

EXPANSION OF THE "FRENCH WOMEN DON'T" SERIES

Internal Publishing Memo

In light of the success of *French Women Don't Get Fat: The Secret of Eating for Pleasure* and its follow-up *French Women Don't Get Facelifts: The Secret of Aging with Style and Attitude*, the series will be expanded in 2018 with the following titles:

Older Danish Women Don't Mind Looking Leathery: The Secret to Having Five Weeks' Paid Vacation Days and Virtually No Melanin

With a charming blend of Nordic wit and insight, Lærke Pederson observes that Americans live in the only wealthy nation that doesn't require employers to provide paid vacation time. This, Pederson explains, is why American women are so pale and sad.

Italian Women Don't Tiger-Mom Their Boys: The Secret of Mixing a Stagnant Economy with a Fiercely Family-Oriented Culture

Concetta Olivieri describes the joys of having her forty-three-year-old son live at home with her. She berates American women for banishing their male offspring when they are so young and incapable of doing their own laundry, just so that they can go off and wear tennis shoes while eating rubbery, orange cheese squares.

British Women Don't Want an Honest Answer to the Question "How Are You?": The Secret of Living in a Culture That Commends Repression

Anna Perks, the author of Collywobbles in Bedfordshire, *reveals why emotions are unfortunate and best left unacknowledged. She hopes that by sharing the virtues of British restraint with American women, they will become more self-conscious and aware of the ridiculous nature of their presence.*

Saudi Women Don't Drive: The Secret of Using Religion to Justify Misogyny

Lydia Al-Bishri explores her decision to move to Munich, where she can enjoy the freedoms of the West without bingeing on cronuts and Snickers bars.

Russian Women Don't Fly Commercial Airlines: The Secret of Landing an Oligarch

Sofya Lischenko is generally clueless, but she owns an $88 million penthouse on Central Park West. She advises American women to smile less, particularly as they have so little in life to bring them joy.

Botswanan Women Don't Worry: The Secret to Being Happier Than You

Mma Ramotswe explains why American women should feel ashamed for being so rich and unfulfilled all at the same time.

Finnish Women Don't Pay for Child Care: The Secret to Living in a Country Where Politicians Actually Legislate Pro-Family Policies

Siiri Lyytikäinen notes that in addition to never being happy, American women will also never "have it all."

No, Jamaican Women Don't Cry: The Secret to Being More Relaxed Than You

Violet Walker is mystified that American women are not only rich, unhappy and unfulfilled, but also so anxious about everything.

Indian Women Don't Sweat the Small Stuff: The Secret to Accepting Yourself Just as You Are

Priyanka Sharma wonders why American women even bother to read books on the subjects of being thin and happy, when it's so clearly and internationally established that they have no chance of being either.

Kazakh Women Don't Remember Borat: The Secret to Resting Assured That No Matter How Socially Divided and Landlocked You Are, American Women Are Still More Unhappy Than You

Lyudmila Baktybayeva dispels the notion that everyone isn't laughing at American women for being so fat and unhappy. They are.

Cypriot Women Don't Deposit: The Secret of Being Overexposed to Greek Bonds

Elena Constantinou highlights why she's taken a series of domestic jobs once reserved for Sri Lankans. But even with all her troubles, she assures readers that she's still having better sex than American women.

Brazilian Women Don't Wear Tops: The Secret to Being Young, Beautiful and Skinny

"Grazielle" rented out her favela home for the World Cup and the Olympics. She is much more beautiful than you.

Colombian Women Don't Mind Being the Sexiest Women in the World: The Secret to Being Young, Beautiful and Skinny According to MissTravel.com

Lucia Ortiz had a boob job but was more beautiful than you even before she had it done.

American Women Don't Feel Good About Themselves: The Secret to Thinking Everyone Else Is Younger, Skinnier and More Beautiful Than You

Twenty-five years after her seminal book The Beauty Myth, *Naomi Wolf is exasperated and applying for French citizenship.*

✦ ✦ ✦

Interesting Little Princess Fact #10

In October 2016, the Walt Disney Company issued a list of "Princess Principles," which outlined how to be a modern-day princess. But instead of letting men from the 1930s and 1940s decide what would be included on the list, they wisely consulted a panel of five thousand parents. Here's the new, official list:

10 Principles of Being a Modern Princess

1. Care for others

2. Live healthily

3. Don't judge a book by its cover

4. Be honest

5. Be a friend you can trust

6. Believe in yourself

7. Right wrongs

8. Try your best

9. Be loyal

10. Never give up

✦ ✦ ✦

Little Princess Pie

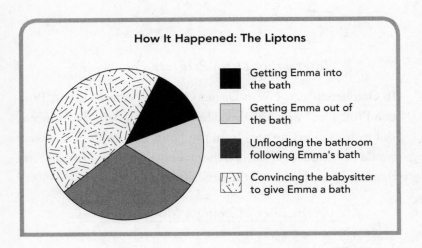

Emma Lipton once went three weeks without a bath. It was one of those things where everyone pretended they didn't know. Emma's mother told herself that Emma's father had probably given her a bath when she wasn't paying attention. Emma's father started to stay at work late in order to avoid bathtime. After being asked to give Emma a bath every night, the babysitter quit.

During summer months, the Liptons took Emma swimming once a week and decided that counted as a bath. But then winter came. Finally the Liptons bought a Princess Ariel Bath Castle and a Barbie Splash'n Spray Water Park as well as all the Disney Princess Petal Float dolls. Since then, Emma has agreed to get into the bath. She still screams when they try to get her out, though.

Chapter 11

LOVE . . . OF COURSE! LOVE!

My Life in Pink:
**THE *FROZEN* FILES, PART 4—WHY
ELSA RETURNED**

Time for one last Little Princess Pop Quiz. Everyone pick up your pencils. Circle the correct answer.

1. ***Cinderella and Prince Charming love each other.***

    A. True

    B. False

    C. How the hell am I supposed to know?

The answer is "C." Cinderella and Prince Charming dance at the ball and go for a walk in the garden. That's the extent of their relationship. They could love one another. They could like one another. They could each be mistaking the other for an attractive hedgehog. Who can tell?

2. *Snow White and the other Prince Charming love each other.*

    A. True

    B. False

    C. How the hell am I supposed to know?

"C" is again the correct answer. The two crazy kids meet at a wishing well and then Snow White runs away. The next thing the prince knows, S. White is dead and he's kissing her in her coffin. Do they love each other? Or is this just weird, disguised necrophilia?

3. *Elsa and Anna love each other.*

    A. True

    B. So true

    C. Girl, you know it's true

Answer: Elsa loves Anna so much that after she hurts her, she hides her magical powers and grows up alone and isolated. Anna loves Elsa so much that she forgives Elsa for hurting her, and then she gives up her only chance to stay alive to save her.

Everyone put down your pencils.

Disney's Sleepy Trio aren't bad because they're love stories or because their narrative is "man saves woman." Even though that's an unreconstructed story, it still works from a storytelling perspective. Like in *Pretty Woman*. Or *Titanic*. Or *Deuce Bigalow: Male Gigolo*.

The reason the Trio films are so weak isn't the presence of love— it's the flimsy portrayal of this most transcendent emotion. The love

portrayed in these movies isn't credible. I know it's churlish to critique them—they're old movies and most old movies suck.[1] But the
love is based on idealized perfection rather than the acceptance of
imperfection. "True love" just isn't there.

Is love the answer to everything?

I wish! Sadly, it isn't, because fear and hate win sometimes.
We've all seen it happen. But love is the pillar that holds us steady
during bad times. It's the fuel that gives us courage to weather
storms. In good times, love makes you high. In dark times, love
is the light that gives you hope.

Love doesn't fix anything external. There may be wolves outside the door waiting for our Little Princesses and, much as we'd
like to, we can't make them disappear. We aren't fairy godmoth-
ers, but mothers and fathers without magic wands. The power we
do have, however, is to give our Little Princesses love and acceptance. The wolves are there, but the resilience to face them arises
from a place of self-belief and self-love.

Elsa didn't have a fairy godmother, either. In her time of darkness, she didn't even have a mother or a father. But she did have
a sister who loved her.

In *Frozen*, Elsa leaves society to be her authentic self, and she
believes she'll have to be alone and isolated forever. Anna is the
one who doesn't acquiesce to her sister's isolation. She tells Elsa
she doesn't have to be afraid or alone or hide her magic anymore.
She can return because, though her secret is exposed, she now has
someone who loves and supports her and can help her. Whereas
Elsa thinks she must always remain alone, Anna believes that

---

1 *Singin' in the Rain* and *Casablanca* are exceptions to the rule. If you don't
   believe me about old movies being the worst, try sitting through *Tarzan
   and the Amazons*. Sorry, people who made movies in the 1940s and '50s.

Elsa can express herself fully and still be loved and accepted by others.

That's the power of having someone love you and believe in you. That's the power of true love. Elsa may be the most popular Disney princess ever, but the real hero of Elsa's story is Anna. She knows that when Elsa releases her magic, it doesn't turn her into someone dangerous or hateful—it just makes her real and beautiful. Anna is the hero because love and acceptance, as opposed to fear and hurt, guide her actions.

Anna's most heroic act, however, comes at the end of the film. In the tradition of Snow White and Cinderella and Aurora, this princess can only be saved by an "act of true love." The first time we watch *Frozen*, the viewer knows that this must come from a man. The audience and the characters alike expect it to come from "true love's kiss." But at the critical moment when Anna might be saved by the man's kiss, she chooses to save her sister instead.

That's Anna's act of true love. It doesn't come from a man. It comes from the most beautiful, accessible source. Anna is saved by the act of pure love that comes from deep inside herself, and which she expresses for her sister.

Finally, Disney told it. Love *can* come from a man, but it doesn't have to come from one. Love can come from a child, a mother, a father, a friend, a brother or a sister. And the truest acts of love arise from yourself. Like Reese Witherspoon said, "We save ourselves. Every woman knows it."

In *Frozen*, Elsa represents fear and Anna love. The whole story revolves around love. In the denouement, when Elsa lets go of fear and embraces love, she ends the eternal winter.

And they all lived happily ever after.

Chris Buck, who created and directed *Frozen* along with

Jennifer Lee, described how they adapted *The Snow Queen* by Hans Christian Andersen:

> We took the original theme from the original *Snow Queen*, and that was love conquers negativity. And for us the negativity for today is fear.[2]

I'd say they hit the nail on the head.

2 "D'Frosted—Disney's Journey from Hans Christian Andersen to *Frozen*," *Frozen* Blu-ray bonus feature (2013).

My Life and Pink:
PINK DRESSES AND OPTIMISM

Mari started loving pink at around the same time that Matt and I were planning to move our family from Jerusalem to New York. That move never happened—Matt ended up getting a job in Luxembourg and we moved there instead.

But before we knew about that job offer, we believed we were bound for America. This was also the same time, as readers might recall from chapter 2, that Mari completed her first "gentle hands" sticker chart for not biting other kids. And according to the patron saint of sticker charts—Saint Googly Eye—this meant she was entitled to a reward.

"I want to go to the mall-ie and get a pink dress," she said.

"Really?"

The pink predilection was still new enough for me to be surprised. *How can a two-year-old want a dress instead of a toy?* I thought.

"How about a flashlight?" I suggested. Mari shook her head.

"Or a yummy chocolate pudding?"

Cai would have leapt at this opportunity. Chocolate pudding was the pot of gold at the end of his "peeing in the toilet" sticker charts and also for his "I let my parents sleep past six a.m." sticker charts. Making Cai happy was always a simple affair that involved sugar. But Mari was different.

"I want to go to the mall-ie and get a pink dress," she repeated. She didn't blink. She wouldn't be swayed. She'd earned a prize and she knew exactly what she wanted.

Good Lord, I thought. *She's only two and already she's asking for clothing. What's going to become of this girl?*

Moving your family to a different continent isn't the easiest thing you'll ever do. It involves logistics and an overload of decisions and more types of anxiety than you even knew existed. As our moving date grew closer, a recurring focus for my anxiety was the idea that we'd made the wrong decision. What if America wasn't the right place for us? What if all the negative things I'd been hearing since moving away twenty years earlier were true?

In Israel we received socialized health care—at the time America had nothing. And though my kids weren't exactly eating greens, their diet was fairly healthy. From afar, it seemed as though American kids were being raised on a diet of processed cheese and sugar-coated everything. Friends who had made the same move warned me of the relentless commercialization. There were ads on the soles of shoes and on people's foreheads. No matter where you went, someone was trying to sell you something. If you had a daughter, that something was most likely pink.

This is the culture we would soon be adopting, and here was my two-year-old, asking for a pink dress. I feared princess culture and yet we were leading her directly into its nerve center.

Where is this going to end? I thought.

Meanwhile, six-year-old Cai had started asking me about America. One of his recurring questions was, "What was your favorite in America? Devil Dogs or Ring Dings?"

The question perfectly combined two subjects that compelled him at that age—"favorite things" and the snacks of my childhood. On a visit to New York the previous summer, I had pointed out those packaged treats of my youth on supermarket shelves and he was instantly fascinated.

The answer was actually Yodels, but Cai got me thinking

about a different version of that question. What was my favorite thing about America?

I left America when I was twenty-one. What made me leave the country in which I was raised? I had many reasons I could list at the time, but in retrospect the one that really drove me away was the feeling that I didn't fit in. My adolescent sense of alienation never left me and I associated my disaffection with American culture rather than what really caused it—my depressive mind, and my tendency to see everything negatively.

Only once I'd left did I understand how American I really was. It wasn't just the cultural references—it was a way of thinking. I believed in fairness. That isn't to say America is the fairest in the land, because it's not, but the idea of fairness is part of the American narrative. I also believed in equality and in hope. Again, America doesn't always exemplify these ideals. But though we fall short, we believe that living in an egalitarian, hopeful society is what we're supposed to be doing. While it's not the reality, it is the purported goal.

I took Mari to the mall to get her sticker chart prize. She did something for the first time that she would repeat on future shopping trips. She walked into the store, headed directly over to the dress she wanted, plucked it from the hanger and said it was the one.

"Are you sure? Don't you want to look around?" I said.

Never in my life have I exhibited that kind of certainty in a clothing store. I thought her age was simply making her rash and that she might not understand what she was doing. Now I know better—that's the way Mari shops. She knows instantly what she wants.

It was a pink sundress with a little buttercup flower print

design and a tulle tutu skirt. After we purchased it, Mari did something else that also ended up becoming her habit every time we shopped. The dress never made it into the shopping bag. She took it from the cashier and put it on immediately, then went to a full-length mirror in the store and started dancing.

I watched her, smiling. What else could I do? I wasn't alone, either. Other shoppers looked over to where Mari was dancing and were also smiling. She's little and adorable and it's a cute dress.

As I enjoyed the show, I knew it wasn't the dress making everyone happy. Kids who dance in public spaces without any awareness that there's a world around them in which such behavior is usually frowned upon are emanating a light. They're bringing enthusiasm and love into the moment in a way adults are no longer able to do.

And then I remembered my favorite thing about America. Optimism.

When you read travel guides written for foreigners visiting the United States, they say that the archetypal American characteristic is optimism. After more than twenty years living as an ex-pat, I believe that's true.

Growing up in New York, I didn't tune into it, but it was there. When I was living with depression and struggling to climb out and looking into myself to find some reserve from which to draw, I think the side of me that finally responded was the American. Perhaps it's not deeply rooted—three of my grandparents were born in Poland. Still, I was born and raised in America and was fortunate enough not to have suffered in my own life. America, with its upbeat spirit and lemonade-making ethos, is also part of me.

I'm a depressive who has managed—with medication years

ago and now with exercise, meditation and mindfulness—to become a lighter person. But I'll never change my nature. Negative thoughts are often my starting point, like the way I was thinking about our move to America, or about buying a little girl a new dress that she'd earned by overcoming her own demons.

"You look beautiful," I told Mari as she danced. I'd feared that this dress would be the start of something destructive. But really, it was the start of something else—my daughter was growing up, and she was learning how to express herself with words and dance and uninhibited emotion.

I think that's the moment when I started to look at pink differently. Before Mari came into my life, pink was the color of feminine weakness. Pink was the loss of spark that happens to girls when they reach adolescence. Pink was all the damaging expectations of perfection and beauty that undermine us and chip away at our spirit. Pink was vulnerability and insecurity and everything that's wrong with being a girl and a woman.

Pink was the color of fear. All the fears I had for my daughter compressed into one soft, innocent color.

Mari had no such fear. For her, pink was the color she loved. There was no baggage weighing it down, because she wasn't carrying any yet. Pink was the focal point for her expressions of fun. Pink was her enthusiasm, her joy and her uncomplicated, beautiful, sparkling love of life.

As Mari danced in her new dress, my heart filled with love and in that space I started to see color through my daughter's eyes. And other things as well.

What if, instead of seeing all the bad things about America, or about any place where we'd end up moving, I could focus on the good? What if, instead of dwelling on the problems of any one society, I could divert my attention to solutions? What if, rather than trying to find a physical country in which I felt I belonged, I instead looked inside myself for that sense of belonging?

And what if, instead of the color of fear, I chose to see pink as the color of optimism?

It was just a tiny shift in perspective, but suddenly everything looked different. Mari finished her dance and ran over to me. I picked her up and hugged her.

"I'm so beautiful!" she said.

"Yes," I said. "You are."

Opposite of Serious

What if, when watching a princess movie, instead of seeing the waist-lines and the flaws in the plotlines, I could instead see that the film might have some redeeming qualities, and something valuable to offer me and my princess-obsessed daughter? That's kind of what this book is about.

While I was in the midst of learning how to see princess films differently, I was also wondering how I could raise a princess-obsessed little girl as a feminist. Since I make fun of stuff, including myself, I wrote a humor piece about my concerns around this subject. Here it is.

Turn Your Princess-Obsessed Toddler into a
Feminist in Eight Easy Steps

1. Read the Brothers Grimm version of "Snow White," in which Snow White is asked to clean, cook, make beds, wash and sew for the dwarfs in exchange for shelter from the evil queen. Ask your toddler to imagine what might have been different if the dwarfs had been female instead of male, and instead of a tiny cottage in the wood, if Snow White had stumbled upon Wellesley College.

2. Wonder aloud, what with Cinderella's history as a cleaner, if she and Prince Charming are likely to share the division of labor in their home. Remark that, if the immaculate state of his white gloves is anything to go by, it's difficult to imagine that he ever takes out the garbage.

3. Speculate whether there is a connection between the Greek mythological Aurora, the goddess of the dawn, who arose from the ocean in a saffron robe and rode her horse-drawn chariot across the sky ahead of the sun, sprinkling dew upon the earth, and the Disney Aurora, who fainted after getting a boo-boo from a spinning wheel and whose prince needed to be rescued by bickering fairies. Decide that no, there's likely no relationship at all.

4. Praise Belle for her love of reading, but segue into a discussion about Stockholm syndrome as it relates to women, and how that might shed insight into the phenomenon of women who stay in toxic relationships.

5. Propose that the hatred that Anastasia and Drizella feel toward Cinderella is not the fault of the stepsisters, so much as it represents a complete indictment of Western society and its attitudes toward feminine beauty. Suggest that all three women might be victims of the same impossible societal pressures. Work in this timeless Naomi Wolf gem: "The contemporary ravages of the beauty backlash are destroying women physically and depleting us psychologically."

6. Chuckle about the patriarchal shenanigans of King Triton. Before the laughter subsides, ask why, in fact, everyone was so threatened by the idea of Ursula the sea witch becoming ruler, when it's clear that she was extremely capable. Point out why Ursula might have valid reasons for becoming so frustrated about the glass ceiling under the sea. Finally, concede that while it's very nice that Ariel and Eric were able to marry, it's too bad that King Triton had the final say over Ariel's body in deciding whether she would be a fish or a human being.

7. Note the similarities between Princess Jasmine and Emma Woodhouse. Point out that if all the energy that went into finding the "right man" was instead diverted to, say, solving global warming or participating in government office—something impossible in Jane Austen's day but well within your daughter's reach—then we would all be so much better off. Here you might want to bake cupcakes in honor of International Women's Day.

8. Make a list of wishes your daughter might ask to be granted from her fairy godmother. When the list is completed, tap your daughter's forehead gently and then say excitedly: "I found your fairy godmother! It's your brain and she's been right here all along!"

Congratulations! Your Princess Toddler is now a feminist. What were you so worried about? Once you speak logically to a toddler, the toddler always listens. Next up: How to Toilet Train the Willful Child in Twenty-four Hours While on an Overseas Trip.

✦   ✦   ✦

Interesting Little Princess Fact #11

Elsa was a villain in an early version of *Frozen*. Snow White's character is fourteen years old. Aurora has just eighteen lines of dialogue in *Sleeping Beauty*. Tiana is the only Disney princess with a job.

Want more of these babies? Google "Disney princess facts" and go to town. It's endless, just like princess merchandise.

✦ ✦ ✦

Chapter 12

HAPPILY EVER AFTER

Our Lives in Pink:
HOW TO RAISE EMPOWERED GIRLS

Here it is. The ultimate guide for how to raise empowered girls.
Are you ready? Steady? Spaghetti!!!

Don't hold your breath!

Thanks for the spoiler alert, Femmie. She's right, of course.
What a notion. The goal of raising well-adjusted, confident children is the elusive chimera of parenting. Because sadly, this stuff

doesn't come in a bottle, even if that bottle is twenty years of sensible child-rearing practices.

I almost fell into the trap of writing this chapter with a voice of certainty. I started making a list of my own recommendations, and then I asked friends and colleagues for theirs. I kept a record of all the wisdom and strategies and websites and books and the kinds of progressive engineering toys that produce female astronauts and neurophysicists and CEOs who earn as much as their male peers. I did this in order to pen this fabulous section for you, dear reader, so that you too may raise an empowered girl.

I won't keep the info a secret—I will post everything on my website—but neither will I pretend that any of it is guaranteed. Some of the advice is obvious and some is informative and helpful. Yet sadly, there is no recipe for us parents.[1]

The funny thing is that a few parents recommended books I'd read as a child, like the *Little House* series and *Pippi Longstocking* and Judy Blume's books. While I enjoyed all of them, no piece of children's literature could stand between me and my falling into an abyss of self-negation and depression. To my great surprise, I had actually followed some of the "empowerment" regime, yet, as my history of depression attests, I was anything but empowered.

My parents are not at fault. They were loving and did a great job. They had their own insecurities, but doesn't everybody? My mother's father lost his whole family in the Holocaust. The enormity of that tragedy informed the way he and my grandmother lived and loved and raised their children. They were grieving and mistrustful and felt (with justification) that we were living in a

---

1 As for my empowered girl, she finally stopped insisting on wearing her tutu every day, but that's just because many of her dresses incorporate the tutu in the design.

hostile and hate-filled world. My father's parents were immigrants who did whatever they could to lift their family out of poverty and into suburbia. Given where they came from and how they were raised, I see how much my parents overcame in order to raise me and my brother and sister in a safe and secure environment.

They were terrific parents and yet they couldn't save me from depression. And if I'm genetically predisposed for it, I know it could happen to my kids.

So what do I do now?

In the first chapter of this book, I asked if brain matter mattered. Now it's time to ask, "Do parents matter?"

In 1998, a researcher named Judith Rich Harris published *The Nurture Assumption: Why Children Turn Out the Way They Do*. The book made a convincing case for why parents don't significantly affect how their children develop. Instead, peers and social environment have a much greater effect than parents in determining what kind of adults they become.[2]

Genes also determine much of who we are. "Twin studies," like the Minnesota Twin Family Study, indicate that genes, aside from determining eye and hair color, play a huge role in personality development. A famous secret research project, done on twin girls separated at birth in New York City, found that even though the mothers of the girls had contrasting temperaments and related to their adopted daughters quite differently, the girls shared similar habits like nail-biting and social insecurity. Eventually the girls grew up and found each other and discovered they

---

2 So let's all pack our bags, leave the kids behind and move to Barcelona! Drinks are on me.

had much in common and even shared the same favorite film, a Wim Wenders movie that is more or less about two alienated souls finding each other.

What can we learn from all this? That's right. "Secret research projects" are always creepy. Once upon a time, psychologists believed they should *separate twins at birth* and then study them without ever revealing to their subjects that they were twins. That's frowned upon now, by the way. Hooray for the breakdown of accepted societal assumptions.[3]

Back to parental influence. From twin studies we know how consequential genes—as opposed to what parents do or don't do—are in determining how a person develops. Yet we also know that genetic power is limited to percentages. There are genes that predispose you to develop Alzheimer's disease, for example. Apolipoprotein E (APOE) is the gene most commonly associated with late-onset Alzheimer's disease.[4] If you inherit this gene from one parent, your risk of developing Alzheimer's is increased. If you inherit it from both, your risk is even greater. Yet everyone who has two of these genes doesn't develop Alzheimer's.

The way we develop depends not only on our genes, but on how our genes interact with environment. And environment = parents + some other stuff. So yes, parents do matter. In terms of our kids, there *is* a percentage of their development still up for grabs. They have talents that can be nurtured or discouraged.

---

3 Yes—that's a reference to the patriarchy. Only in a patriarchal society would twins be separated at birth and then subjected to a secret study in the name of science.

4 J. Kim et al., "The role of apolipoprotein E in Alzheimer's disease," *Neuron* 63, no. 3 (2009) and J. T. Yu et al., "Apolipoprotein E in Alzheimer's disease: An update," *Annual Review of Neuroscience* 37 (2014).

They have potential that can be realized or untapped. They have predispositions that can flourish or wither, depending on what happens in their lives.

So, sorry—we can't collectively move to Barcelona just yet. But neither can we pretend that we have control over what happens to our kids. We don't. We never did.

Does that thought make you cry sometimes?

In a time of trouble my BFF Amy once told me, "You do the best that you can do at the time that you do it." I love the compassion of this sentiment. It's true of most parents, in most circumstances, forever. We do our best on any given day yet the impact of our efforts depends on variables that are out of our control.

If Brené Brown and other social scientists are correct, and the ability to feel connected to others is what gives meaning and purpose to our lives, then at the very least we can cultivate our connection to our children. We can be with them and love them as life unfolds. There are no guarantees. But compassion and support and love can soften the harsh edges of reality. And if you ever feel guilty about any of it—the things you didn't do, the things you couldn't buy, the things you bought even though you shouldn't have, the things you forgot, the messes, the meals you didn't cook, the sugar consumed, the hours you were at work, the activities not signed up for, the moving of houses, the moving of schools, the marital strife or the divorce or the single-parent status, the siblings you provided and didn't provide and the sibling fights you mishandled, the tears when you left them with a babysitter, the minutes you spent hiding in your bedroom as someone called, "Mommy! Mommy! Mommy!"—just make a list of everything. Remember all those mistakes and write them down. Be thorough. Now take the piece of paper and burn it and then go hug your child. Because it turns out we aren't the potter's wheel after all.

So I offer this resource with a grain of salt. All the recommendations from other parents along with a few of my own are on my website. It's there for you to peruse if you feel the need or if you feel like some company, but if you don't, then trust that instinct. Because though I can't promise you an empowered girl, I can promise that you are the exact right parent for your child.

And in about twenty years, I'll see you in Barcelona. Drinks are on me.

Their Lives in Pink:
LITTLE PRINCESSES SPEAK

Once upon a time, little girls dreamed of becoming princesses.

Of course they did!

Until relatively recently, the only way for a woman to have stuff like a comfortable life or power or a tiara was to marry someone who could provide those things for her. Marrying the right man was crucial. Marrying a prince was the brass ring.

Those days are gone for middle-class women. We can buy our own $625 titanium corkscrew[5] if we feel like throwing good money down the toilet. We can build our own castles and run for president and even wear a rhinestone-encrusted headpiece whenever the mood strikes us. Consequently little girls don't dream of marrying princes anymore. They just dream of *being* princesses

---

5 Actually a thing. There's also a custom-made titanium corkscrew that costs $70,000.

for the sake of being princesses. So where does that leave *our* Little Princesses?

If the full-scale marketing of princesses to little girls only began in 2000 when Disney launched the princess line, this means that the first generation of girls to fall under the princess merchandising spell are coming of age now. Who are these girls and where are they now? What do they make of their princess obsession now that they're young adults? Are they embarrassed? Bemused? Nostalgic about their days in pink? Are they still twirling in tutus or are they all dressed in goth? What has become of the first generation of Little Princesses?

In the spring of 2016, I sent out a survey asking teenagers and young women who once identified as "princess-obsessed little girls" to describe their experience. Here they are. Meet the Little Princesses who were the first to fall down the Disney princess merchandising rabbit hole. They're an interesting bunch. This is what they said.

What's your name and how old are you?

Hally, 19	Mariah, 17
Vanessa, 17	Rina, 17
Stephanie, 18	Avara, 18
Jennifer, 18	Rachel S., 18
Julia, 18	Liliana, 18
Sarah, 16	Atara, 17
Michelle, 17	Tzivia, 16
Ruth, 17	Rachel C., 16
Eliana, 17	

Do you remember when and how your princess obsession started?

HALLY: I loved princesses for as long as I can remember. It started when I was obsessed with Madeleine the French girl when I was three, and she isn't really a princess or Disney, but she paved the way for me to love Pocahontas and Ariel.

VANESSA: When I was two, I was attracted to blingy tiaras.

STEPHANIE: I started loving princesses when I was probably four. I don't know how it started.

JENNIFER: My obsession started in kindergarten. My older sister introduced the Disney films to me.

JULIA: Obsession started around age three and I remember it started because my parents read me fairy tales before I went to sleep every night.

SARAH: My princess obsession probably started when I was three or four. Not sure how.

MICHELLE: I began to love princesses around the age of four. I don't remember exactly how it started, but I had these small, sparkly figurines that I took everywhere with me.

RUTH: My princess obsession must've started young, as in three years old kind of thing. I don't remember exactly how it started, but I was told many fairy tales and played with a lot of princess dolls, so I'm sure that helped things along.

ELIANA: I have been obsessed with princesses ever since I can remember. It started when I first watched *The Little Mermaid* and blossomed into a lifelong obsession with all princesses.

MARIAH: I wouldn't say I'm obsessed, but it started when I first saw *Beauty and the Beast*, so I guess I was four.

RINA: Started at age three when I was shown Disney movies, particularly *Mulan*, *Pocahontas*, and *The Little Mermaid*.

AVARA: I started my princess obsession around the age of three and it started because I saw the movie *Beauty and the Beast*.

RACHEL S.: My princess obsession started before I was able to remember. My parents would put on the Disney movies for me and I loved singing/music so I would always sing the princess songs. I guess that's how I got into the princesses.

LILIANA: My obsession started when I was around seven. I remember it started when I watched Disney movies. They inspired me to become like them.

ATARA: Probably around four or five years old. It probably started with Barbie dolls.

TZIVIA: My princess obsession started when I was very young, probably four. I think the true inspiration for my obsession began with Princess Jasmine. She was so much prettier and cooler than all of the others—she was different.

What do you remember about your princess- and pink-loving days?

HALLY: When I was four and we moved to a new house, I wanted a unicorn rainbow fairy princess wallpaper, but my dad made me get regular pink instead. I also used to sing princess songs in the shower and played all the parts. I never really liked to dress up, but everything I owned was pink.

VANESSA: I was so obsessed with princesses that the first time I ever visited Disney World I threw a fit until my mom took me to dinner with the princesses. Also, when my brothers were mean to me I threw the plastic high heels at them.

STEPHANIE: I was a princess for Halloween from the ages of four to eight. I've always loved the color pink and it was my favorite color for a very long time.

JENNIFER: I wore a Snow White costume for weeks on end and for my birthday in winter. I once ripped up a VHS tape of *Mulan* to get back at my sister for taking it away from me all the time.

JULIA: I was a fairy princess for five years straight on Halloween. I had a wand and I would desperately try to change people's minds to do what I wanted them to do.

SARAH: My room was covered in pink from head to toe. I had everything with princesses: clothes, Barbies, all the movies, etc.

MICHELLE: I remember being fascinated by princesses! I loved to read books, watch the movies and dress up.

RUTH: I mostly remember that, for a few years, people stopped asking me what my favorite color was; it was a given that it was pink. When my favorite color finally did change, I was the one who went out of the way to inform people of the groundbreaking news, since the people around me had continued to assume my pink obsession was simply ongoing. Also, during my princess phase, I had my youngest cousin fully convinced I was a real princess. He believed it for a bit too long, if we're being honest.

ELIANA: When I was about six years old I had a toy dining set and a bunch of princess dolls. I used to set up tea parties between my stuffed animals and princesses. One day I got really jealous of my princess doll, because she was having so much fun at her tea party, so I sat in her beach chair (which then cracked), put on her sunglasses (which then bent) and put on her flip-flops (which only fit my pinky toe) and then I lay down in the sun trying to make her jealous. My mother walked into my room and couldn't stop laughing at the sight of me.

MARIAH: I remember being so attached to the idea that I was a princess, and I was always wearing those little pink plastic princess high heels just about everywhere my mother took me no matter the weather.

RINA: My dad and I used to play games where I was Mulan or Ariel and he'd pretend to be Shang and Eric and rescue me from danger. I remember getting a whole box of princess dresses and shoes to match them and being mad that I had to wait until Purim to wear them.

AVARA: I would always dress up in full princess gear—a pink dress, crown, fake jewels, etc. . . . The funniest story is when I wore my princess outfit on vacation to Disney World and on the plane there, I complained about being in the way back of the plane (coach) and the flight attendant was able to move me and Dad to sit up in the front because "that's what nice princesses get."

RACHEL S.: I would always want to dress myself in crazy outfits. I would scream and cry if my mom picked out an outfit for me because I wanted to create my own princess look. For my seventh or eighth birthday I had it at a gymnastics place and my mom got me a cute sporty outfit, but I only wanted to wear this bright furry jacket and a giant tutu. I also remember crying and begging my mom to make sure my new room was pink when they announced that we were moving.

LILIANA: I remember that I always wanted to buy Disney princesses. My mom would also buy everything pink for me.

ATARA: I used to love a game called Pretty Pretty Princess. I remember there was jewelry and shoes. I also had a phase where I rode a decked-out pink bike featuring My Little Pony and sparkly images, with frilly strings attached on both ends of the handlebar.

TZIVIA: I remember dressing up. A lot. Sometimes for no reason.

RACHEL C.: I had all the princess gowns (Cinderella, Snow White, Sleeping Beauty and Belle) in a blue hamper, along with accessories, and I loved dressing up in them. My favorite princess was Sleeping Beauty, until my brother told me that she was stupid, so I switched to Belle . . . I remember once I was in Disney World, dressed all in pink, and the one thing I wanted was to see Aurora, but we had no luck. Finally, my family found a secluded area to relax and eat a snack. And there Aurora was . . . coming out of the bathroom. But I took a picture with her, and it's still on my shelf in my room.

On the reaction of parents, family and friends:

HALLY: I was my daddy's little girl so he loved all of it. My brother hated it, though.

VANESSA: My mom loved and encouraged it by buying me all of the princess costumes since I was the only girl in the family.

STEPHANIE: As far as I remember they were all supportive.

JENNIFER: My parents thought it was hilarious.

JULIA: My parents weren't concerned because I was young and just gravitating toward an outlet that allowed me to expand my imagination.

SARAH: Everyone thought it was cute!

MICHELLE: I am the oldest daughter and the first grandchild, so everyone was so happy that I loved pink and girly things.

RUTH: I remember that my younger brothers weren't exactly huge fans of the times when I tried to dress them up and put makeup on them like pretty princesses.

ELIANA: I have two older brothers who are eleven years older than me, so growing up I was constantly surrounded by all their friends. The ladies loved it and thought I was adorable, so my brothers used to take me out a lot with them to pick up girls.

RINA: My parents were supportive. Maybe I was made fun of by some of the boys in my grade, but I'm not sure.

AVARA: They would all laugh and smile at me. They called me their cute little princess. I was their joy and only girl in the family at the time.

RACHEL S.: When I was younger people *loved* how obsessed I was with princesses. I remember my older cousins would quiz me and try to trip me up, because I knew the princesses so well. I think with the exception of how clearly I wanted to do things on my own and how outspoken I was, I kind of fell into the cliché princess-loving/pink-obsessed girl.

LILIANA: Everyone knew that I loved princesses, so they always knew what to get me.

RACHEL C.: My mom was a closeted princess-obsessed child, but she was too embarrassed to let it show. So when I became that way, she got really into it and had lots of fun buying the dresses for me. Everyone else wasn't bothered by it, but I quelled the obsession a bit when I was with my dad and turned to things like cars and running.

Did your princess obsession end? At what age?

HALLY: Probably when I started middle school, but it never really went away, which can be seen by the fact that I watched *Frozen* in theaters four times.

VANESSA: It has not and never will end.

STEPHANIE: Around age ten maybe.

JENNIFER: My obsession ended at the end of elementary school.

JULIA: Yes—it ended around age eleven.

SARAH: I still love princesses. I love to rewatch *Beauty and the Beast* and all those amazing movies. But I think it probably ended when I was in, like, second grade . . .

MICHELLE: Yes, probably by age six or seven.

RUTH: I would say my princess obsession must've ended around the time I was in first grade or so, but the idea of being a princess, in terms of holding oneself up to a certain standard, is something that has continued to influence different aspects of my life.

ELIANA: My princess obsession hasn't ended, but definitely died down once I got into middle school.

MARIAH: Probably when I turned eight. Princesses and pink were out, and Game Boys and baby blue were the new fad.

RINA: Ended around age eight.

AVARA: I stopped pretending to be a princess around the age of six or seven.

RACHEL S.: My princess obsession has not ended. It has definitely subsided, but I still go to Disney and wait on those lines to meet them. I also think I'm less focused on the actual princesses and more toward their stories.

LILIANA: My obsession ended once I started middle school when I was eleven.

ATARA: It definitely ended before I was ten years old, but I'm not really sure.

TZIVIA: Probably when school started giving homework.

What are your interests now? Is there a career or job you're pursuing or planning to pursue?

HALLY: I'm majoring in international studies, and I have always wanted to travel, which could be an extension of my desire to live in the far-off worlds the princesses lived in.

VANESSA: I'm going to Cornell University in the fall and plan to become a lawyer.

STEPHANIE: I love theater and I used to figure skate. I'm in college right now and I hope to become an elementary school teacher.

JENNIFER: I really enjoy writing and hope to go into the publishing field.

JULIA: Pursuing a job in the STEM fields for realistic reasons, despite the fact that I prefer the arts. I hope to study biology/genetics in college with a minor in English and pursue a job either working in a lab or teaching at an institute.

SARAH: I love to read. I love science (especially chemistry). I'm definitely going to pursue a job with medicine.

MICHELLE: I am very interested in science and medicine, and I am going to college next year and studying premed. I have wanted to be a doctor my whole life.

RUTH: I've always enjoyed reading and writing. Right now, I don't have a particular career I'm planning on pursuing.

ELIANA: I'm interested in a whole bunch of things. I like to draw, paint and write. I hope to travel the world one day and experience life to the fullest. I don't have any career preferences in mind, but I don't want to hate my job. I want to be happy—that's my one true goal in life.

MARIAH: A princess. Just kidding! I plan on studying history and either becoming a professor or a lawyer.

RINA: Writing and singing. I want to become both a professional singer/performer and an author.

AVARA: I'm interested in journalism, the entertainment industry, TV, film, Broadway, etc. I'm planning on pursuing a career as a reporter for the entertainment and Broadway industry, as well as working as a casting director.

RACHEL S.: I love to work with children. I grew up acting/singing/performing and I'm currently a theater major in college with the intent of getting a master's in education, but I definitely want to make a career as a theater or elementary education teacher.

LILIANA: My interest now is art. I am going to an art college so that I can pursue Disney animations.

ATARA: Behavioral therapist. I want to help children overcome behavioral obstacles, such as twitching, hair pulling, etc. . . .

TZIVIA: I love writing.

RACHEL C.: I like reading and sports. I'm planning to pursue a career in publishing.

How do you view your enthusiasm for pink and princesses all these years later?

HALLY: I still love everything Disney and magical, so I view it in a positive light.

VANESSA: I think my experience with princesses was positive and brought joy into my childhood years.

JENNIFER: I think it was an enjoyable and typical childhood phase.

JULIA: I view it as harmless and natural.

SARAH: I think it was totally normal and cute for a little girl to be obsessed with pink and princesses.

MICHELLE: I think it is cute! I feel like most little girls loved princesses.

RUTH: Clearly, I'm not still playing dress-up with tiaras and plastic pearls. That being said, pink is still a pretty color and frankly, it's fun, when you're all dressed up or doing something that makes you feel powerful, to think of yourself as some sort of ruler-princess person who has the power to change the world.

ELIANA: As a child being obsessed with pink and princesses is normal.

MARIAH: I laugh at myself.

RINA: I view it as having been healthy. It was more of a slight infatuation than obsession. When it comes to obsessions I tend to think more of *Harry Potter*, *Star Wars*, etc.

AVARA: It's a very low level of enthusiasm now. I do still love to watch princess movies, but I'm way more critical of them. Pink isn't my favorite color anymore. I grew out of princesses.

RACHEL S.: I love how much I love princesses. It gets me excited and motivated and I love how it made my childhood interesting. So many stories came out of my obsession. It fostered my creativity and got me excited about something.

LILIANA: Now princesses don't really excite me. I also became tired of the color pink.

ATARA: Pink definitely does not dominate my perception of the color spectrum, however, I am fond of pastel pinks.

TZIVIA: Pink has always been my favorite color.

RACHEL C.: Sometimes, I'm embarrassed about all the money that was spent on princess-related items for my youth, but in general, I had a lot of fun so I don't regret the obsession.

Do you think your early interest in pink and princesses had any lasting negative effect on you?

HALLY: No, I think that all the uproar about body images and waiting for your prince to come find you are just women looking back on the tales as adults. As a child, you don't think about that stuff. Yes, I wanted to find my Prince Charming, but I viewed the princesses as active and I thought I could go out and find him, not wait in a tower. Also the princesses seemed like adults when I was young so I didn't compare my body to theirs; besides, they weren't real people, just cartoons, so obviously I wouldn't look like them.

STEPHANIE: I don't think so.

JENNIFER: No.

JULIA: When I became older I felt a pressure to be ashamed of my interest because it was immature and not realistic.

SARAH: I don't think it had a negative effect at all.

MICHELLE: Negative? Nope! To me it was simply a phase of childhood.

RUTH: Of course, princesses could have negative connotations in terms of being saved by the prince or not being able to take care of things themselves. However, as long as you think of yourself as the type of princess who can be her own hero, and can save the day even while wearing high heels, there shouldn't be a negative effect from princesses. That's how I choose to view princesses and that's why I don't think my early interest in pink and princesses had a lasting negative effect on me.

ELIANA: I don't think it had a negative effect on me, but I do think that most of the princesses I was raised to idolize were very thin and had perfect everything. I was a very chubby child, so at the time I wanted to look just like those princesses, which brought down my confidence a lot as a child, because the bodies they portray are almost impossible to obtain.

MARIAH: I don't like the color anymore. To me it signifies a girl that needs to be saved, and not a capable person who can do it herself. The color also makes me feel like a piece of bubble gum— only worth five cents, and loses flavor quickly.

RINA: Any lasting negative effect? No, but it's harder for me to like pink now because of society's idea that it's a "girly" color that represents weakness.

AVARA: It made it harder to realize that growing up—life—isn't a princess/Disney film. There isn't going to be a prince to save you. I learned that I'm going to have to do stuff for myself, if I want to see an outcome. I learned that I didn't need a prince to save me. I was very reluctant to accept that fairy tales are only stories.

RACHEL S.: I do think that since I was classified at such a young age as "girly" it has kind of been a stereotype that I feel like I need to either fall into or escape. I don't dress girly anymore— leggings and a comfy shirt—to kind of counteract the fact that I do have "girly" interests and a high-pitched voice. I also think that I feel like I constantly need to try to act more mature because I do love something that is childish.

LILIANA: No, there was no lasting negative effect.

ATARA: No.

TZIVIA: Nope.

Do you think your early interest in pink and princesses had any lasting effect on you—positive or otherwise?

HALLY: I read a lot, and I almost exclusively like fantasy and historical books. I like to read about far-off lands and things that could never happen to me. I enjoy the escape from reality, which I think comes from how much I used to get absorbed into the lives of princesses and fairy tales.

VANESSA: I think my experience with princesses has led me to view myself as a princess. I try to always act with class and hold myself to a higher standard. Also, being a princess taught me the value of a kind heart.

STEPHANIE: I have a very vivid imagination so it could have played a role.

JENNIFER: I think it did positively in the sense that my favorite princesses were ones like Mulan who fought for honor and respect and that taught me a lot about being mature and making sacrifices.

JULIA: I just think I had a good time and I'm glad I realized that although some fairy tales portray weak women, princesses can still be strong.

SARAH: I think it opened up my imagination that anything is possible.

RUTH: I think my early interest in pink and princesses had a positive effect on me in the way that when you think of yourself as the type of princess who has the power to do what she wants and rule the kingdom and do all that, you think of yourself on a higher level and about holding yourself up to a certain level. This "level" may be different for everyone, but the implication that you can possess unique abilities and you're a special individual makes you keep your head up and not let the world, telling you to be a certain way, get you down.

ELIANA: My love for princesses definitely had a positive effect on me. Each and every princess comes with a life lesson that always applies no matter the age. Belle teaches you not to judge a book by its cover. Mulan taught me that it's okay to pursue what I love no matter what society thinks. Ariel taught me to be bold and chase after what I love, and Cinderella taught me that everything works out in the end.

RINA: Made me feel happy and pretty at the time.

AVARA: It made me appreciate how I was able to play pretend. Children these days are so in touch with technology that playing pretend is uncool, so I'm happy that I got to experience playing dress-up and pretend. It also made me realize that children do learn from everything they see and hear. They're very responsive. So many things these days give us unrealistic presentations of how things truly are in life and that's dangerous to teach kids "this is how life is." It's made me more aware of the hardships in life.

RACHEL S.: Yes! I think it has given me an outlet to be creative and has also helped instill a sense of optimism in me.

LILIANA: I believe that princesses allowed me to express myself. I looked up to them and they were all special in their own way. Therefore, I think that it had a positive effect because it encouraged me to be myself.

TZIVIA: I learned many important life lessons and morals from princesses. For my English class this year, I even wrote a paper defending the values of Disney princesses.

RACHEL C.: Yes. One of my main relaxation methods is watching *Sofia the First* with my mom. Anything princess related makes me smile. I was even surprised to find myself really excited for all those new live-action adaptations of princess movies!

What do you recommend to parents who have princess-obsessed little girls?

HALLY: To encourage them. From a child's perspective, princesses lead fun and exciting lives. Fairy tales exist in a world when there is justice in the end, which ensures them to make the world a better place. Princesses also help them use their imagination, which is important when you are young. If princesses and pink make your daughter happy, encourage them because once they grow up, the lessons they learn and the happiness they remember will make them stronger and better people.

VANESSA: Let them flourish and dream, but also make sure they stay grounded.

STEPHANIE: I would let her do whatever she wants. It could be a phase and if not, I don't think it really matters. Just let her know that she doesn't need to be saved by a prince to be a princess.

JENNIFER: Let them live it out, but keep them away from idolizing the princesses.

JULIA: Let them have fun and let them enjoy their childhood.

SARAH: Let them run with their obsession, and enjoy it while it lasts. Let them live in a make-believe world where there are princesses and happiness.

MICHELLE: Let them play and be creative!

RUTH: Instead of shutting down the idea of princesses, as being made up and just part of a patriarchal society, emphasize the good parts of princesses. As much as you can say princesses are antifeminist or anything else, you can also say that princesses also send positive messages. Parents should emphasize that there is no one specific kind of princess, any girl can and should be her unique self. Further, parents should clarify that girls don't need the prince to save them. Girls can always have the power to save themselves, and can wear poofy pink dresses while doing so if they choose to.

ELIANA: Any girl that is princess obsessed should be allowed to let it shine through them. Nowadays with all the rapid growth of technology it's rare to find a child that even knows any old-time princesses like Cinderella or have even heard of Mickey Mouse. Let your children be exposed to the world of pretty dresses and beautiful princesses waiting for their Prince Charming. It's better than having them stuck to their tablet.

MARIAH: Well, first I'd ask them if their daughter showed interest before becoming obsessed. I think that the true test to see if it's something their child actually loves is to show them some *Bob the Builder*, and let them choose what they want to love from there, instead of abiding to social norms.

RINA: Let them be obsessed with princesses. Squelching their interests will only lead to resentment.

AVARA: I would say that they need to tell their kids that princesses and how princesses act in the movies is nothing like real life. They must distinguish between pretend and reality to their child. They also shouldn't spoil their children that are obsessed with princesses because it could come out to be that the child is very spoiled and thinks that they deserve everything later in life.

RACHEL S.: Give them the freedom to explore that—let them choose their outfits (even if it means you getting dirty looks when people see your kid dressed in something outrageous). Let them tell the stories and sing the songs. It will help them figure out their likes and dislikes and give them the confidence to be creative. I would say to steer them away from the aspect of the princess waiting for/needing a prince. We're way past that and there are so many other positive aspects of the princesses.

LILIANA: I recommend for parents to continue to encourage little girls to become like princesses. They should allow their girls to like whatever they are interested in.

ATARA: Don't spoil them rotten, but definitely let them play games equivalent to Pretty Pretty Princess and dress-up.

TZIVIA: Let them obsess, but also know which lessons to absorb.

RACHEL C.: Leave them be. They're having fun, and when it comes to children, nothing lasts forever.

Afterword

PRINCESSES AND WOLVES

I never thought I would defend Disney princesses. I'm the woman who makes fun of them. I'm the gal who laughs at my daughter's propensity to dress like a garish, Southern belle–inspired lounge singer. I'm the parent who laments my failure to banish pink and princesses from my home.

But, as with parenting in general, I learn as I go. As Mari's obsession swelled to comic proportions, I separated the princesses from what was actually generating my anxiety—that my daughter would follow in my footsteps, that she would lose her spark and confidence.

I can't ensure this will never happen to her. But I am certain of the following:

- Trying to control children will harm and not help them. Being controlling is worse than princesses.

- Fear is also worse than princesses.

- Fearing shame, and not letting yourself be vulnerable and authentic, is worse than princesses.

- Approaching everything with negativity is worse than princesses.

- The pressure put on girls and women to be perfect is worse than princesses.

- Lots of things are worse than princesses. Come to think of it, why was I ever even worried about princesses? They are frivolous and fluffy at times, but they certainly aren't menacing.

We parent our children for a finite number of years, and then they go into the forest, where there are extraordinary wonders but also wolves that will block, badger, threaten and, yes, sorry to say, hurt them. There are the upsetting wolves, like the beauty industry and the expectations of perfection and a culture of shame and a consumer industry that will forever try to convince us that we need more, rather than accept and be grateful for what we have. And there are the dangerous wolves, like sexism and misogyny and sexual assault. It's all out there. We can't make the wolves disappear.

The Serenity Prayer goes like this:[1]

> *God, grant me the serenity to accept the things I cannot change,*
> *Courage to change the things I can,*
> *And wisdom to know the difference.*

Accepting your children, surrendering to the chaos of parenthood, and loving them just as they are, flaws and all, doesn't make

---

1 American theologian Reinhold Niebuhr wrote this prayer.

the wolves disappear. But it can give them resilience. It can give them the serenity, courage and wisdom they need to face the world. Our Little Princesses may soon stop loving princesses and pink, or they may turn thirty by throwing themselves a princess-themed party with Glass Slipper cocktails.[2] Who knows? That's really up to them. Either way, our job is to accept them, prepare them for the forest and love them. We don't have control over what happens. That's parenthood. That's pretty much everything.

I think the reason we have kids is that when they come into our lives, they immediately demonstrate that life is messy. They arrive in this world covered in greasy gook. They spit up and burp and poop and pee in our faces. In those first few months, our homes smell like sour milk and look like appalling squalor. Yet within this relentless chaos, a parent may feel more elated and at peace than ever before. Though you're suddenly spending all your time with the most vulnerable and demanding human being you've ever met, you may find that you're also filled with the most love and compassion you've ever felt before. Surely this is the meaning of parenting. It comes to teach us acceptance. It allows us to experience that magical alchemy, in which we take that impulse of fear and resistance and clutching on to something for dear life, and we let it go.

---

2 Really a thing!

ACKNOWLEDGMENTS

I would like to thank my fairy godmother, Jody Kahn, for sprinkling her fairy dust talents and belief onto this book at every stage. Many thanks also to my editor Sara Carder and her excellent team at TarcherPerigee/Penguin. FunFact: They also publish *The Artist's Way*, so I'll just go ahead and thank them on behalf of all writers everywhere. Thanks to my parents and sister, Adena, and to Malkie A. and Amy K. for always being so supportive of my writing—sounds like a small thank-you, but to writers, encouragement is more valuable than all the exploitable riches of Arendelle. Thank you, Binders, to whom I owe a debt of gratitude for helping me get where I wanted to go.

Thanks to all the editors who published the humor over the years that appeared in this book: K. J. Dell'antonia at the *New York Times*, Chris Monks at *McSweeney's Internet Tendency*, Larry Carlat at *Purple Clover*, Sarah Breger at *The Forward*, and also to Akashic Books, *The Hairpin*, *Mommyish*, the *Huffington Post*, and the fabulous feminist Establishment.co team. A special thank-you to the *New York Times* for granting permission to reprint my humor pieces that originally appeared on its parenting blog, *Motherlode*.

Thank you to the young women who participated in my Little Princess survey, both for taking the time to share your experience but also for helping to allay my fears because you all seem pretty cool and smart and grounded despite all the pink lurking in your collective Disney-obsessed pasts.

Speaking of which, thank you, of course, to Elsa and Anna and to all the other Princesses—you crazy, tulle-wearing, perfect pitch singing, beauty ideal–perpetuating things, you. To some extent, you're all part of the problem, but if everything were perfect then I'd have nothing to write about. Also, it's not like any of you ever killed anybody, right?

Right?

Thanks to my husband/partner/main squeeze, Matt Rees—we are rockin' this whole fixer-upper thing.

Notes

Chapter 1

"Quiz: Are You a Little Princess Toddler?" originally appeared in the *Huffington Post* as "Quiz: Are You a Princess-Obsessed Toddler?".

"And I know it's totally crazy to think I'd find romance!" is a lyric from "For the First Time in Forever," music and lyrics by Kristen Anderson-Lopez and Robert Lopez, from *Frozen: Original Motion Picture Soundtrack*, Walt Disney Records (2013).

Chapter 2

"What Would They Do?" originally appeared as part of AkashicBooks .com's Terrible Twosdays series.

Chapter 3

"Holiday Gifts for Little Princesses" originally appeared in the *Huffington Post* as "What I Want for My Princess-Obsessed Toddler vs. What My Relatives Will Get."

"Free-Range vs. Helicopter Parenting: Get the Facts" originally appeared in the *New York Times Motherlode*.

"The Unmonitored Baby Is Not Worth Having" originally appeared in the *New York Times Motherlode*.

Chapter 4

"A Woman's Attempt to Accept Herself Goes Awry" originally appeared in *Purple Clover* (www.purpleclover.com) as "Accepting Yourself Is Hard to Do."

Chapter 5

"Top 10 Rejected *Sofia the First* Plotlines" originally appeared in *Mommyish* (www.mommyish.com) as "10 *Sofia the First* Plot Lines That Would Make the Show Bearable for Parents."

"Top 10 Ways to Make Disney Collector Your Friend" originally appeared in the *Huffington Post*.

Chapter 6

"Conceal, don't feel / don't let them know / Well, now they know" is a lyric from "Let It Go," music and lyrics by Kristen Anderson-Lopez and Robert Lopez, from *Frozen: Original Motion Picture Soundtrack*, Walt Disney Records (2013).

"No right, no wrong, no rules for me. I'm free!" is a lyric from "Let It Go," music and lyrics by Kristen Anderson-Lopez and Robert Lopez, from *Frozen: Original Motion Picture Soundtrack*, Walt Disney Records (2013).

Chapter 8

"Study on Household Inequality Sheds Light on Flying Fruit Epidemic" originally appeared in *The Establishment* (www.theestablishment.co) as "Household Inequity Causes Flying Fruit Epidemic."

"Notes for My Husband During My Overnight Trip" originally appeared in the *Huffington Post*.

Chapter 9

"Working Mothers Have More Successful Daughters, According to Recent Depressing Study" originally appeared in the *Forward Sisterhood Blog* (www.forward.com).

"20 Ways to Erode a First-Time Mom's Self-Esteem" originally appeared in the *Huffington Post*.

Chapter 10
"Expansion of the 'French Women Don't' Series" originally appeared in *The Hairpin* (https://thehairpin.com).

"Yes I'm alone, but I'm alone and free" is a lyric from "Let It Go," music and lyrics by Kristen Anderson-Lopez and Robert Lopez, from *Frozen: Original Motion Picture Soundtrack*, Walt Disney Records (2013).

Chapter 11
"Love . . . Of course! Love!" is a line of dialogue from *Frozen*, Walt Disney Animation Studios; directed by Chris Buck, Jennifer Lee; produced by Peter Del Vecho; screenplay by Jennifer Lee; story by Chris Buck, Jennifer Lee, Shane Morris. Burbank, Calif.: Walt Disney Pictures, 2013.

"Turn Your Princess-Obsessed Toddler into a Feminist in Eight Easy Steps" originally appeared in the *New York Times Motherlode*.

About the Author

Devorah Blachor's writing has appeared in the *New York Times*, *McSweeney's*, *The Rumpus*, *Redbook*, and *Good Housekeeping*. She wrote the *New York Times Motherlode* parenting column "Diary of an International Move." Under the pen name Jasmine Schwartz, she wrote the mystery novels *Farbissen* and *Fakakt* about a thirty-something New Yorker whose search for herself is constantly interrupted by the discovery of dead bodies. She lives in Luxembourg with her husband and their two children.